FOR KING AND COUI

Family Motto: It is lawful to repel force with force.

FOR KING AND COUNTRY

A Tribute to Three Brothers

Eric	Henry	John
Gwynne-James	Gwynne-James	Gwynne-James
1893-1916	1896-1959	1903-1944

by
David Gwynne-James

REAL LIVES PUBLISHING

First published in Great Britain in 2006
by Real Lives Publishing,

ISBN 10: 0-9550050-1-9
ISBN 13: 978-0-9550050-1-5
EAN: 9780955005015

A CIP catalogue record for this book is available from the British Library

Book and cover design: Alan Hamp
Index: Ingrid Lock

Printed and bound in England by
Biddles Ltd, King's Lynn, Norfolk

MM VI REPELLERE LICET

This book is dedicated to
the Gwynne-James family
and their descendants

Contents

Illustrations   8

CHAPTER 1 **Introduction**   11
           Appendix

CHAPTER 2 **Eric Gwynne-James**   21
           Early life; First World War;
           Appendices; Family Recollections

CHAPTER 3 **Henry Gwynne-James**   53
           Early life; First World War;
           Between the Wars; Second World War;
           Victory in Europe;
           Appendices; Family Recollections

CHAPTER 4 **John Gwynne-James**   123
           Early life; Pre War Service;
           Second World War;
           Appendices; Family Recollections

CHAPTER 5 **Reflections**   197
           Field of Remembrance;
           Family Acknowledgements;
           Sources & References

           Notes   209
           Index   212

Illustrations

Introduction
1. The family tree.
2. Mrs Sophie Gwynne-James with her eight children.
3. Aylestone Hill, Hereford, 7th May 1912.
4. The Drawing Room at Aylestone Hill.
5. Tonacombe Manor, Morwenstowe, North Cornwall. Looking down 'the Street'.
6. The Hall, Tonacombe Manor.
7. Tidnacott, Morwenstowe, North Cornwall.
8. Mary as a Red Cross Nurse during the First World War.
9. Frank and Sophie Gwynne-James on their Golden Wedding Day.

Eric Gwynne-James
10. Lord James's letter to Eric at Cheltenham College, 6th October 1909.
11. Lord James of Hereford with his Great Nephews, Eric and Henry.
12. The Cricket Bowling Dragon won by Eric at Cheltenham College in 1911.
13. Eric at Oriel College, Oxford.
14. Oriel College Rugby Union Football Club 1912–1913.
15. Eric with his mother in the garden at Aylestone Hill.
16. Post Card. The British Army in France.
17. Sketch Map: Hooge 9th August 1915.
18. Officers of the 1st Battalion KSLI in France in July 1916.
19. A 'C' Company Mark 1 Tank, Chimpanzee Valley 15th September 1916.
20. The 1st Battalion leaving the trenches near Ginchy in 1916.
21. Post Card: Hospital at Rouen in 1916.
22. Eric's grave at St Sever Cemetery, Rouen.
23. The First World War Memorial in the Chapel Cloisters at Cheltenham College.
24. Plaque in the nave of Cheltenham College Chapel.
25. Silver statuettes of KSLI Buglers and helmet badges, 85th King's Light Infantry.
26. The Family Grave at Tupsley, Hereford.

Henry Gwynne-James
27. Prince Albert at RNC Dartmouth, 1912.
28. Henry as a Midshipman with his mother outside Aylestone Hill.
29. HMS *Collingwood*.
30. Prince Albert by 12 in Gun HMS *Collingwood*, 1913.
31. Fabric from Lieutenant Culley's Sopwith Camel; HMS *Redoubt* 1918.
32. HMS *Temeraire*.
33. Christmas Card 1920–21 to Henry from Prince Albert.

34. Henry, Mary and John at Tidnacott, 1921.
35. HMS *Stormcloud* 1925.
36. Henry with his ship's company, HMS *Stormcloud*, China Seas 1927.
37. Henry with his mother and her father, Bill Waddon Martyn .
38. Henry holds June atop a stone pillar at Tidnacott, 1929.
39. HMS *Antelope* at port in the Mediterranean .
40. Henry leaves Aylestone Hill to command RN Barracks, Chatham May 1932.
41. HMS *Fearless*.
42. Henry's telegram of congratulations from His Majesty, King George Vl.
43. Henry at the German Club, Shanghai on German National Day, 1939.
44. Henry hands over to Lieutenant Commander Sheppard, October 1940.
45. HMS *Capetown* at Nancowry in the Nicobar Islands.
46. Henry on the Quarter Deck of HMS *Capetown* in the Indian Ocean.
47. Hole in HMS *Capetown* viewed from dockside looking forward.
48. His Majesty's letter to Henry dated 3rd February 1942.
49. Force G landing craft at Southampton, 1st June 1944.
50. Landing craft loaded on to transporters at Nijmegen.
51. Landing craft being unloaded on the banks of the Rhine.
52. Naval landing craft form the first completed bridge in the British sector, 1945.
53. Henry and his Staff study a map of the Rhine battle area at the base.
54. Captain P Henry Gwynne-James RN.

John Gwynne-James
55. John batting at RMC Sandhurst, August 1923.
56. John in civilian clothes wearing an Old Cheltonian tie.
57. John with his mother at Aylestone Hill, 1927.
58. Jalapahar in Bengal, where John met Anne on 28th May 1928.
59. Anne at Clovelly, August 1929.
60. John and Anne at Tidnacott, August 1929.
61. John carrying June, his niece at Aylestone Hill, 1929.
62. John with Biddy, July 1930.
63. John with his mother at Aylestone Hill, July 1931.
64. Anne on her engagement to John in 1933.
65. Anne carrying Davina in Colchester days.
66. John with Davina and David in the garden at Littlegates.
67. Propaganda leaflet dropped by German aircraft in May 1940.
68. John as Lieutenant Colonel with his son, David, and his father Frank in 1942.
69. John as Commanding Officer with the Bugle Platoon KSLI in 1942.
70. Sketch Map: The Advance from Medjez, Tunisia 23rd April–6th May 1943.
71. Soldiers of 1 KSLI beside a knocked out German tank in Tebourba on 8th May 1943.
72. John as Brigadier addressing some NCOs after cessation of hostilities in Tunisia.
73. Sketch Map: Island of Pantellaria showing coastal defences.
74. Surrender Conference at Pantellaria on 11th June 1943.
75. Admiral Pavesi and his Chief of Staff. John is behind and to the left of the Admiral.
76. Sketch Map: Stalemate in Italy, December 1943.
77. Sketch Map: The Landing at Anzio on 22nd and 23rd January 1944.

78. Sketch Map: The Advance to Campoleone, 29th–30th January 1944.
79. Sketch Map: German counter attack forces withdrawal 3rd–4th February 1944.
80. Sketch Map: Fourth Battle of Cassino, Fifth and Eighth Armies break through.
81. Sketch Map: Rome to Lake Trasimene.
82 Sketch Map: Villastrada to Vaiano, 20th–21st June 1944.
83. Sketch Map: Pescia River to Spina River, 24th–1st July 1944.
84. Sketch Map: Details of Troop Movements, Pescia River, 24th June–29th June 1944.
85. Investiture at Buckingham Palace for John's DSO, on 17th July 1945.
86. Oil portrait of Brigadier John Gwynne-James DSO.
87. John's grave in the Commonwealth Cemetery at Orvieto, Italy.
88. Orvieto Cathedral town, 1959.

Reflections
89. The KSLI plot at The Field of Remembrance 2003.

Photographic Acknowledgements

I would like to thank the following for providing photographs and maps and for permission to reproduce copyright material. While every effort has been made to trace and acknowledge all copyright holders, I would like to apologise should there have been any errors or omissions.

Country Life, 11th November 1933; 5, 6. IWM Department of Printed Books, Official History of the War: Military Operations France & Belgium 1915; 17. Pantellaria. The Reduction of Pantellaria and Adjacent Island 8th May–14th June 1943 Army Air Force History Study; 73. The Trasimene Line June–July 1944 by Janet Kinrade Dethick; 82, 83, 84. IWM Photographic Archive (with negative numbers); 19 (Q5574), 49 (A23731), 50 (A27836), 51 (A27815), 52 (A27816), 53 (A27827), 71 (NA2605), 72 (NA14222), 75 (NA3590). National Archives, Kew; 29, 32, 41, 47. The King's Shropshire Light Infantry 1881–1968 by Peter Duckers for The Shropshire Regimental Museum; 18, 20. Cheltenham College The Development Office; 23, 24. David Mansell Photography; 25, 86. 1st Battalion The King's Shropshire Light Infantry Campaign Service 1939–1945, Compiled by Lieutenant Colonel R Evans MC and Major Maurice E Jones Late KSLI; 67, 69. The First Division in Action Tunisia 1943; 70. Anzio by Wynford Vaughan-Thomas; 76, 78, 79. Alex The Life of Field Marshal Earl Alexander of Tunis by Nigel Nicholson; 77. Cassino Portrait of a Battle by Fred Majdalany; 80. Algiers to Austria A History of the 78th Division in the Second World War by Cyril Ray; 81.

CHAPTER 1

Introduction

FOR MOST OF MY LIFE I have been aware of an inherent pride in the history of the Gwynne-James Family based in Hereford. In particular this pride relates to several generations, many of whom entered the legal profession and achieved great distinction during their careers. Not only was the firm of Gwynne-James & Sons, Solicitors, a much respected family firm in Hereford for 150 years, but we could count among our forebears a Peer and Cabinet Minister, a County Court Judge and three Mayors of Hereford, one Recorder and two Registrars. As can be seen from Appendix 1 our family links with Hereford go back to the Eighteenth Century. Initially some of our family were Surgeons but since then most have entered the Legal profession. Our best known member of the family was my great great uncle, Lord James of Hereford (1828–1911), who declined Gladstone's offers of Lord Chancellor and Home Secretary. His life is well chronicled by Lord Askwith in his biography, first published by Ernest Benn Limited in 1930.

During the period covered by this book, the family home of my Grandparents, Frank and Sophie Gwynne-James and their eight children was Aylestone Hill. This Victorian mansion which had a fine garden, enjoyed extensive views both across Hereford and the River Wye towards the Black Mountains.

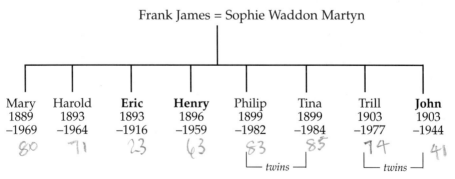

Frank James = Sophie Waddon Martyn

Mary	Harold	**Eric**	**Henry**	Philip	Tina	Trill	**John**
1889	1893	1893	1896	1899	1899	1903	1903
−1969	−1964	−1916	−1959	−1982	−1984	−1977	−1944
80	71	23	63	83	85	74	41

Philip 1899 / Tina 1899 — twins

Trill 1903 / John 1903 — twins

1. The Family Tree

It was to the Drawing Room that Frank, Senior Partner of Gwynne-James & Sons, Solicitors, would have returned after work to join his wife, Sophie and their children. This was a typical well-to-do home of the period for a large family. Six staff also lived on the top floor. The five brothers and three sisters enjoyed a happy and stimulating early life at 'The Hill'. Later on they returned there from their various travels whenever possible to see their parents and catch up with family news.

Their mother, Sophie's family home was Tonacombe Manor, Morwenstowe in North Cornwall. This has been the seat of the Waddon Martyn family since the Seventeenth Century and remains so to this day. This rambling low lying yet compact manor house contains three Courts and a Great Hall with a Minstrels Gallery. It is a remarkable survival of a Cornish Gentleman's House, rather remote among the sunken and twisting lanes leading towards the Atlantic cliffs.

Soon after Sophie married Frank at Lifton Church in 1887, the Gwynne-James family began spending their summer holidays with the Waddon Martyns at Tonacombe. As both families increased it became impossible to accommodate everyone. This was resolved by the Waddon Martyns gifting the land on which the Gwynne-James family then built Tidnacott, their holiday cottage. This became the scene for most family holidays before and between the wars.

However, as is well remembered the first half of the Twentieth Century was blighted by two World Wars within the space of thirty years. Inevitably these wars had a profound and devastating effect on most families. In our family's case most of my grandfather's eight children performed war service in some capacity or another.

During the First World War their eldest daughter, Mary became a Red Cross Nurse and a theatre sister, while their eldest son, Harold served as a Major with one of the headquarter companies of the Welsh Division Army Service Corps in France. Their fourth son, Philip served as a subaltern in the Royal Artillery during the latter stages of the First World War and in France for four months during the first occupation after the Armistice. He also served in the Home Guard throughout the Second World War. John's twin sister, Lilian, who had an excellent singing voice, was nicknamed Trill, following her recitals at various troops concerts. However, *For King and Country* is a specific tribute to three brothers Eric, Henry and John, all of whom had distinguished service careers. Eric and John became soldiers and served in the same regiment, but in different wars. Both died for their country. Henry served in the Royal Navy and survived both wars.

2. Opposite: Mrs Sophie Gwynne-James with her eight children.
Left to right, back row; Philip, Harold and **Eric**. Middle row; Mary with baby Trill, Tina standing, Sophie with baby **John**. In front, **Henry**.

3. Aylestone Hill, Hereford, 7 May 1912.
4. Below: The Drawing Room at Aylestone Hill.
5. Opposite: Tonacombe Manor, Morwenstowe, North Cornwall. Looking down 'the Street'.

First World War (1914–1918)
Eric 1893–1916
Captain Eric Gwynne-James, DSO, 1st Battalion, The King's Shropshire
Light Infantry. He served in France from January 1915 for twenty months,
the last thirteen as Adjutant. In October 1916, aged twenty three, he died of
wounds sustained at the battle of the Somme.

First and Second World Wars (1914–1918 & 1939–1945)
Henry 1896–1959
Captain P Henry Gwynne-James, Royal Navy, and ADC to the King. He
served for thirty four years, from being a Midshipman in HMS *Collingwood*
at the battle of Jutland in 1916 to commanding British Naval Units during
the Crossing of the Rhine in 1945. Unlike his two brothers he survived both
wars, but tuberculosis forced his early retirement aged fifty two in 1948.

Second World War (1939–1945)
John 1903–1944
Brigadier John Gwynne-James DSO. He commanded the 1st Battalion, The
King's Shropshire Light Infantry in North Africa in 1943. As Brigadier he
commanded the 3rd Infantry Brigade during the Assault Landings on the

6. The Hall, Tonacombe Manor.
7. Opposite: Tidnacott, Morwenstowe, North Cornwall.

8. Mary as a Red Cross Nurse during the First World War.
9. Frank and Sophie Gwynne-James on their Golden Wedding Day.

Island of Pantellaria in June 1943 and at Anzio in Italy between January and April 1944. He commanded the 36th Infantry Brigade during the fourth battle of Cassino in May 1944 and during their fiercely fought advance to and North of Rome. He was killed in action near Lake Trasimene, Perugia in June 1944, aged forty.

*   *   *

My grandfather, Frank Gwynne-James, was Senior Partner of Gwynne-James & Sons during the First World War, between the wars and during the Second World War until he died aged eighty six in 1942.

His two solicitor sons, Harold and Philip, followed their father into the family firm. After Harold left the firm in 1936 and when Frank died in 1942, Philip, being then in a 'war reserved occupation' found himself Senior Partner and the only family member in practice. By the time he retired from Gwynne-James & Eland thirty eight years later at the age of eighty in 1980, I was the only male Gwynne-James of the next generation. I had already served thirteen years in my father's regiment, had left the Army and was well settled with Arthur Young & Co (later Ernst & Young) in London. In those days so many young men, almost as a matter of tradition, followed their father into the services. No pressure was exerted in my case, yet it seemed the natural thing to do. My career choices signalled the end of the family connection with the firm after one hundred and fifty years. War devastates and influences the aspirations of subsequent generations.

When serving at home and after I left the Army in 1971, my wife, Charmian, and my mother, Anne and I usually attended the Remembrance Service at the Field of Remembrance at St Margaret's Westminster in November each year. Here we laid crosses in memory of my Father John and my Uncle Eric in the Regimental Plot of the King's Shropshire Light Infantry. In 1986 I decided that I should display the distinguished sets of medals of all three brothers in a cabinet as a tribute to their service for King and Country in both World Wars. As Uncle Henry's medals could not be found, I wrote to the Public Record Office at Kew to obtain his Statement of Service and then to HMS *Centurion* at Gosport to identify the medals he was entitled to wear. The Medals Department at Spink & Son's produced a duplicate set for Henry and an exceptional display cabinet.

Early in 2004, nearly sixty years after my father was killed in 1944, I decided to take the display cabinet tribute to these three brothers a step further by writing their expanded obituaries. Fortunately I had inherited their eldest sister, Mary's Family Scrap Book which bulged with photographs, press cuttings, letters and cards relating to every member of the family. When my mother, Anne died in June 2001, I inherited further papers on my father, John. Since then my cousin, June has passed me several family papers relating to Henry, including the letters he received from his lifelong friend and contemporary Prince Albert, later to become His Majesty King George VI. This family archive, supplemented by reflections from older members of the family and my own interest in the military history provided a useful starting point.

However I soon decided that if future generations are to understand why these brothers were fighting for their country in various parts of the world during this period, their experiences needed to be put into the context of the events of their time. For example, it did not seem appropriate to assume that all readers would know about the battles of Jutland or the Somme in the First World War or about the North African and Italian Campaigns in the Second World War. As a consequence my original concept of three expanded obituaries has been replaced by researched descriptions of the different actions in which the three brothers took part. I have leavened these service career scenes with a snapshot of their early lives and some family recollections on each brother. This is why my tribute to the three brothers has grown from a leaflet into a book.

Personally I have found this need for detailed research fascinating and cathartic. This process has given me a better understanding of the First World War, which I had never studied in any detail before. Researching Eric's military service on the Western Front and Henry's naval service at sea during the First World War has been like completing a jigsaw puzzle of their respective experiences. I have been able to fill some gaps in my previous knowledge regarding my father, John's military service during the Second World War. In Henry's case there have been several fascinating riddles to unravel regarding his inter-war and Second World War service. His career has required more research than his two brothers. I have found my Reader's Ticket to The National Archives at Kew and to the Caird Library at the National Maritime Museum at Greenwich invaluable in tracking his thirty four years service in the Royal Navy.

My hope is that members of our extended family and future generations will enjoy reading this tribute. It is another chapter in our family history of which we can be truly proud. By sketching in their experiences against the wider backdrop of war service operations, this book should help us all understand where they were, what they were doing, what they achieved and what happened to them.

*   *   *

My thanks to my family who have helped and encouraged me throughout the writing and production of this book (see pages 203–204). Finally I am indebted to Alan Hamp for his typesetting, book and cover design skills. As with *Letters from Oman* it has been a delight working together.

Appendix
Gwynne-James Family links with the City of Hereford

1730–1787   Gwynne- James. Surgeon Kington.

1756–1801   Gwynne-James. Surgeon.

1782–1850   John James of Hereford. Solicitor.

1789-1860   Philip Turner James. Surgeon.

1786–1812   Gwynne-James. Surgeon.

1820–1908   John Gwynne-James. Solicitor. Mayor of Hereford 1868 & 1887.

1828–1911   Lord James of Hereford QC.
Solicitor General 1873. Attorney General 1874/1875.
Privy Councillor 1885. MP for Taunton 1869–1885.
MP for Bury 1885–1895.
Attorney General to HRH Prince of Wales and to the Duchy
of Cornwall.
Chancellor of the Duchy of Lancaster.
Baron James of Hereford 1895.
Grand Cross of the Victorian Order.

1855–1936   Sir Arthur Gwynne-James, Barrister at Law.
Recorder of Hereford 1894.
Court Judge 1899.

1856–1942   Francis Reginald James. Solicitor.
Mayor of Hereford 1898.
Registrar of Hereford, Kington, Leominster and Ross
County Court.

1889–1969   Frances Mary James; married The Rev Rowland Walton Rhys MA,
Rector of Mordiford.

1893–1964   Harold Gwynne-James. Solicitor. Hereford.

1820–1980   Gwynne-James & Sons, Solicitors. 150 years.

1899–1982   Philip Gwynne-James. Solicitor. Hereford.
Legal Secretary to the Bishop of Hereford for 40 years.
Registrar of Diocese for 40 years.
Mayor of Hereford 1935 & 1936.
His sister Lilian was Lady Mayoress in 1936. Succeeded his
father as Registrar Hereford, Kington, Leominster, and Ross
County Court retiring in 1971 after 32 years.

CHAPTER 2
Eric Gwynne-James
1893-1916

Early Life

Eric, who was born on 25 August 1893, inherited his mother's golden hair, the only one of her eight children to do so. As he grew up it became clear that this was a rather special youngster of great promise. He seemed to possess a rare balance of good looks, sharp intellect, natural athletic ability and good temperament. This was later crowned by an unusual patience and unassuming charm. His zest for life and genuine straightness were to win him many admirers and much affection at school, university and in the army.

In 1901 at the age of eight he went to boarding school at Moorland House Preparatory School at Heswall in Cheshire. Later he was remembered by the Headmaster, Mr Dobie for his unselfish, patient and gentle temperament as well as his promising all round talents. His early skill as a slow left arm bowler won him his colours in the 1905 Cricket XI.

In the Autumn of 1907 at the age of thirteen Eric became the sixth member (Appendix 2) of the family to go to Cheltenham College, but the only one to win a Lord James of Hereford Bursary. Eric's early scholastic achievement had to be clear cut so as to avoid any whiff of nepotism. Nevertheless it must have been a little daunting for him to know that his uncle, Lord James of Hereford (former President of the Council) headed the Special Committee and another uncle, Judge Arthur Gwynne James was also on the Committee during most of his time at College. Two years later Eric ran short of pocket money and Lord James came to the rescue during one of his regular visits to Balmoral Castle.

No records exist of his academic achievements at Cheltenham College except that he was successful in gaining entry to Oriel College, Oxford. Rather typically of the time, sporting records were better maintained. These show that he was in the College Cricket XI in 1911 and 1912 and won the Bowling Dragon in 1911 for coming top of the bowling averages.

A 1912 newspaper cutting describing the Cheltenham v Haileybury match at Lord's records:

'The two successful bowlers at Lord's were James and Firbank. The former, who easily heads the bowling averages, struck as lacking

10. Lord James's letter to Eric
at Cheltenham College, 6 October 1909.
11. Lord James of Hereford with his Great
Nephews, Eric and Henry.
12. The Cricket Bowling Dragon won by Eric at Cheltenham College in 1911.

variety both in pitch and pace, but his record of 39 wickets for under 19 runs must be accounted as a good performance on this summer's hard and true wickets.'

Three further newspaper cuttings earlier that season record good performances:

v The Incogniti: 'James played a fine innings of 110, containing a 6, a 5, and ten 4's … '

v The Old Cheltonians: 'James carried his bat for a stylish 67'

v Clifton College: 'James played bright cricket for 72 and 38… and took 3 wickets for 25'

Eric was also in the College Rugby XV. Both uncles and all his family must have been proud of him.

As to his time at Oriel College Oxford, photographs record that he was in the College Rugby XV and the Rifle Shooting VIII in 1912.

13. Eric at Oriel College, Oxford.
15. Eric with his mother in the
garden at Aylestone Hill.

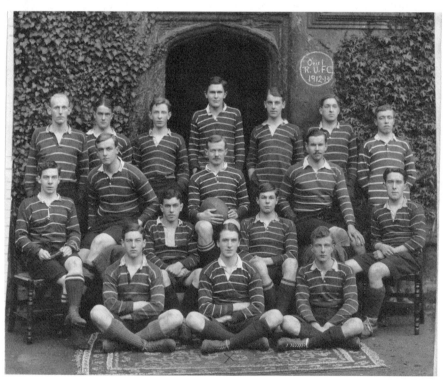

14. Oriel College Rugby Union Football Club 1912–1913. Eric is centre, front row.

He was also in the Oriel College Cricket XI. An extract from a letter from L R Phelps, the Provost of Oriel, to Eric's father on 24 October 1916 soon after he died of wounds, gives a good insight into how Eric had been regarded:

From the moment he came to us we all admired and we all loved him – he was so modest, so unassuming and so 'straight'. I have known few men of these latter days with so much charm; but that is not all – he passed through his time here without a stain upon his character, and I am sure that he was much respected by his contemporaries.'

He was still at Oxford when war broke out and in common with so many of his contemporaries he responded to the first call for men by enlisting in the Army.

First World War

Unless young men expressed a preference to join the Royal Artillery, the Royal Engineers or the Cavalry they were invariably posted to their County Regiment. Eric soon found himself undergoing training as a Rifleman in The King's Shropshire Light Infantry, whose recruitment area included Shropshire and Herefordshire.

After completing his basic training in Shrewsbury he was posted to the 3rd Battalion and commissioned as a Second Lieutenant on 15 August 1914, ten days before his twenty first birthday. In January 1915 he was cross posted to the 1st Battalion, which five months earlier had joined the 16th Brigade of the 6th Division, part of the First Expeditionary Force in France. He and three other new officers joined the battalion on 2nd January, just as it had moved into billets in Armentières for a week's well earned rest. As the town was intermittently shelled during this rest period, this will have been his first experience of enemy artillery fire.

Armentières (January–May 1915)

Eric's first taste of trench warfare was on the 9 January 1915 when the 1st Battalion KSLI relieved the 1st Battalion, The Royal Fusiliers in the trenches at Rue du Bois about a mile and a half south of Armentières. This was an unsettling time to join the battalion. Anecdotes were rife regarding the spontaneous truce, which had started in no man's land on Christmas Day 1914 and had spread into adjoining sectors. This unofficial truce was destined to last into early January. Some extracts from letters written by Captain Guy Goodliffe MC[1] to his wife, describe some scenes during the truce forward of the Royal Fusiliers' trenches, which the KSLI had just occupied:

December 25, 1914

>*I hear that up in the trenches our men and the Germans are walking about arm in arm! There is a mutual trust – one regiment has just sent down for a football so as to have a game with the Germans – isn't it too ridiculous?*
>*To my mind it makes everything look rather silly.*

December 26, 1914

>*Yesterday I did go out and speak to those Germans, but I was unlucky as I only got hold of a very bumptious subaltern who all the while tried to prove to me what a mighty country Germany was. … Later three other German artillery officers came past, and seeing my stars on my sleeve thought I was an NCO. Upon being told by the bumptious subaltern that I was an officer, they all begged my pardon and bowed and saluted. I did likewise!*

December 30, 1914

>*All yesterday and all last night it rained and things were reaching an impasse. The trenches were pretty full of water. In places all the planks were floating about. It was apparently equally bad with the Germans with the result that early this morning both sides climbed out of their trenches and began to bail out for dear life! Everyone was apparently fed up and so had a mutual truce. Isn't it extraordinary? Both ourselves and the Germans just got out and worked on top of the trenches.*

January 6, 1915

>*Still this unofficial truce continues. It makes me laugh to see our men putting up barbed wire in front of our trenches and the old Saxons (the Germans) not paying the slightest attention.*

January 10, 1915

>*All the 7th it poured incessantly and then to make things absolutely impossible our gunners insisted on shelling the German trenches. Everyone was against it except I believe General Paget. All this time our truce with the Saxons continued. We were forbidden to hold conversations with them but by a sort of mutual agreement neither side fired. We did our best to warn them to get back into their trenches as we knew our gunners were going to fire and the gunners also gave them every chance. But it was not because of the truce that we complained but because we would be shelled in return and we knew that our trenches were awful to be shelled in. Sure enough the Germans shelled back and I had a very narrow shave.*

Opposite: 16. Post Card. The British Army in France.

An extract from a letter from Captain Guy Goodliffe describes the appalling conditions in the trenches shortly before handover to the KSLI.

January 12, 1915
Armentières billets.

> *I am going to give you some idea of what life in the trenches was like. Each day it rained more or less and each day the trenches became worse and worse. It was not only the rain falling in the trenches but the water percolating through the sides and also the main springs bubbling up from the bottom. It took two days to compel me to evacuate my first position. We could not keep the water under, so we dug a fresh trench behind – very shallow with a high parapet – but even that soon began to fill and we had to bale out with buckets and tins. We placed innumerable planks on the floor, but still it became worse and worse. Then we evacuated part of the trench. These bits of trench that we evacuated were dammed up and gradually became three or four feet deep in water. So finally, we were holding islands everywhere. We had of course a communicating trench running back, but this soon became impassable as it was several feet deep in water and mud. Also all the sides began to fall in and now I don't think anyone could go down it. That was the state of the trenches when we left them.*

Due to this protracted period of incessant rain, which had been largely instrumental in causing the truce, the trenches which the KSLI now occupied were in a very bad state. Consequently during slightly improved weather the men were put to work to reclaim long stretches that had been abandoned and flooded. Because the Germans were doing the same, the battalion was able to complete a strenuous fortnight's work largely uninterrupted and were able hand over the trenches to the York & Lancaster Regiment in a much improved state.

By mid January the unofficial truce was over, yet the aftermath resulted in the first five months of 1915 becoming a comparatively quiet period for most units including the KSLI. Even so Eric and his colleagues in the Rifle Companies will have been acutely aware that between January and May, the battalion had lost 36 killed and 61 wounded. A steady flow of drafts from England were needed to keep the battalion up to strength. Because poisonous gas had been used by the Germans during their attack on the Ypres Salient on April 22 all ranks had been issued with respirators and had received gas training.

Ypres Salient (June 1915–July 1916)

On June 1st the three battalions of 16th Brigade – 1st Bn KSLI, 1st Bn The Buffs and 2nd Bn York & Lancaster Regiment – and the remainder of 6th Division, moved to the Ypres Salient. This was to remain their theatre of operations for the next fourteen months. Here troops settled into a protracted period of attritional trench warfare, often under appalling conditions in a largely featureless landscape. This demanded discipline, resourcefulness, bravery, stamina, resilience and a sense of humour. Both sides were continually probing for weaknesses to exploit in their enemy's front line and were directing machine gun and artillery fire to defend their positions.

Relatively short periods of intense fighting were interspersed with longer periods of routine. Yet much energy and resourcefulness were needed to maintain and improve the trenches and perimeter defences and to keep the troops well fed and as comfortable as possible in all circumstances. Because of the static nature of trench warfare, lack of exercise tended to make the troops unfit for marching long distances. Waterlogged trenches caused trench foot and the bitter cold, chronic rheumatism. Consequently in order to keep troops fit to fight, periods in the trenches seldom exceeded ten days. The length of time in the trenches would be adjusted to take account of the current threat, a unit's casualties, and an assessment of fatigue, morale and the prevailing weather conditions. On relief, troops would often march quite long distances back to billets or rest camps to get out of the range of enemy artillery. Two diary entries by Captain Goodliffe describe the night occupation of the trenches and the state of soldiers when relieved:

January 14, 1915

It is a wonderful sight to walk up to the trenches from behind. You pass all the skeletons of houses that have been shelled to little bits and see in front of you the line of fires that mark the trench positions. And here there is a great beam of searchlight lighting up the country. You have to watch it and lie down if the beam comes your way. Then now and then you see a sort of rocket sent up to light up a bit of the country at night where someone has a panic or has heard something suspicious; but I miss the singing we had in our other trenches. We used to sing and the Germans applaud. Then they had a turn and you could hear everyone clapping. They had one right good singer too – a great favourite with our men. He was known as 'Opera'.

January 16, 1915

There is no doubt about it that trench life wears one out. You would look with pitying eyes on the men now as they march along having been relieved in the trenches. None of the swinging arms or martial tread. None of the smartness of uniform and appearance that you normally see. Only a sort of herd of men clad in all sorts of odd garments with blankets and sheepskin coats, sacks of charcoal and all sorts of odds and ends. And so they go by dragging their feet – there's

*no keeping step. Some of them limping – most of them with holes in their kit,
all filthy dirty with mud and blackened faces. And yet their spirit is the same.
They joke and laugh as always, but they couldn't march far now, poor devils.*

Eric's experiences during his fourteen months with the KSLI in the Ypres
Salient will have been similar to many of those serving with other units.
However, from *The History of The KSLI in The Great War 1914-1918* I have
selected some extracts of actions and incidents in which Eric would have
been closely involved.

Hooge. *August 8 and 9, 1915* On 5th August the KSLI relieved the 6th
Somerset Light Infantry in the trenches at Hooge. Here the line had been
badly knocked about and the trenches were in a bad state. On the 8th
August during a reconnaissance of the enemy's trenches, the Adjutant,
Captain Hoffmeister was seriously wounded. Lieutenant E G James took
over as Adjutant.

At 3.15 am on August 9th, 16th Brigade mounted an attack on a 1000
yard front, KSLI on the right and 2nd York & Lancaster on the left. All
previously lost ground was regained and held against desperate counter
attacks. An important spur north of the Menin Road was won and
consolidated. KSLI received great praise for this action which was held as
a model of close cooperation between infantry and artillery. This action
came at a cost of 58 killed, 229 wounded and 18 missing.

La Brique. *December 17, 18 and 19, 1915* On 16th December the KSLI
relieved 8th King's Royal Rifle Corps at La Brique. Continual bad
weather had made the trenches very dilapidated and in need of a great
deal of work. There was heavy German shelling on 17th and 18th and at
5.15 am on 19th there was a German gas attack. Our troops had prior
warning. Phosgene was used for the first time. A strong North East wind
carried the gas across the salient as far South as Ypres-Commines.
Casualties were light among the troops in the line, who used gas helmets,
but heavier casualties occurred as far back as Poperinghe. The German
attack on the KSLI front started with heavy shelling followed by gas. It
was a complete failure in the face of gallant and cool defence. Men were
full of fight and sang in the trenches. Casualties 6 killed and 14 wounded.
Casualties by gas 4 killed and 43 suffering from the effects.

Shortly after this action, and on 23 December 1915, Eric was mentioned in
despatches for distinguished and gallant conduct in the field. During Eric's
time at the front, which would have been interspersed with periods of rest
and recuperation in the reserve and some home leave, he sent many cards

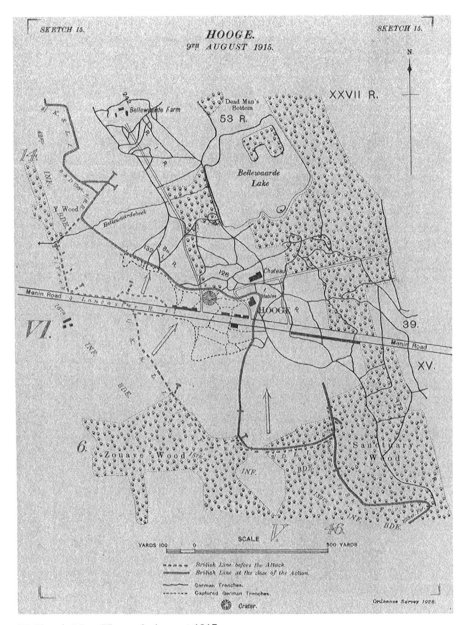

17. Sketch Map: Hooge 9 August 1915.

and letters home to members of the family. Many of his cards were sent to his younger sister, Tina, who wrote frequently to him from St George's School, Ascot. Only one of Eric's letters still exists today and this was written while home on leave to his younger brother Henry, serving with the

Royal Navy. This delightful letter, shown at Appendix 2, portrays his affection for his older sister, Mary and a ready sense of humour.

A further extract from *The History of the KSLI in the Great War 1914–1918* describes a memorable action in which Eric was involved:

Chateau des Trois Tours. April 21 and 22, 1916 On 16th April the KSLI relieved the Buffs in trenches at Chateau des Trois Tours. On April 19th the enemy attacked after an extensive bombardment and captured a portion of trenches at Morteldje Estaminet. On the night of 21st the KSLI counter attacked and with great difficulty and in appalling conditions regained all lost trenches. The mud was so deep the men had to crawl almost flat throwing their rifles in front of them. Some wounded men in the centre suffocated in the mud. Nevertheless courage and devotion to duty had won through. During intense bombardment on 22nd, Lieutenant Colonel Luard was severely wounded and died on the 24th. Major B E Murray DSO took over command. Decorations awarded for action during the night April 21/22 included 1 DSO, 2 MCs, 9 MMs and 1 DCM.[2] Casualties 25 killed, 140 wounded and 6 missing.

Here is this same action as described in an extract from the Daily Telegraph of 1 May 1916:

GALLANT SHROPSHIRES
BRILLIANT NIGHT ATTACK

By PHILIP GIBBS
WITH THE BRITISH ARMIES IN THE FIELD, April 25

The King's Shropshire Light Infantry have the names of many great battles on their Colours, as those of Nieuport and Salamanca, and the Shropshire lads, country born and country bred, who have followed the plough down the big brown furrows of our English soil, have fought on many fields in Europe before this war. The old stock has not weakened. A few days ago – on the night of April 21 – they proved themselves again to have very stout hearts and steady nerves, not afraid of obstacles which would have spoilt the fighting spirit of men less brave.

It was not a great action in which they were engaged. It was nothing more than the retaking of a captured trench, and in this war such incidents will hardly find a record. But the marvel of it was the courage of the men, a courage which made them stick to a job almost hopeless in its difficulties, and carry it through to success by sheer will-power. Imagine what it was like to assault that position which had been taken from us by the enemy on April 19 along the Ypres-Langemarck road. When the Shropshires left their own trenches in the night there was a heavy downpour of rain, and they had in front of them a great quagmire, through which they would have to wade in order to reach the enemy's wire.

The ground had been churned up by shell fire. High explosives had dug out craters everywhere, very deep and filled to the brim with mud and water. Old communication trenches had been smashed up, and had become a welter of earth, with rain-filled gullies. The day of storm had flooded all this bit of country and made the soil beneath a soft bog, in which men sank here and there up to their arm-pits. Well might their hearts have sunk when they began to flounder in front of the enemy's guns. But the Shropshire lads struggled on. To prevent themselves from sinking they lay flat on the mud, and pushed themselves along with hands and knees, throwing their rifles in front as they gained each yard, or using them as poles to support them in the slime. A few fell into shell craters, and were drowned. Some were so caught and stuck by the mud that they could not get free nor move a yard. The assaulting companies all struggling like this lost touch with each other in the darkness, but pressed forward independently to their objectives. The men on the right, or as many as could keep together, rushed the enemy 's trenches at about half past one in the morning, and took possession of a portion of it in spite of heavy rifle fire, grenade, and machine-gunfire from the enemy's support trenches. Bombing parties worked up further and established posts, but could find no sign of the men who had been advancing with them on the left. At first it seemed as though the men here were alone in the enemy's lines, but later cheering was heard, which showed that the centre of the assault had also reached their objective through the quagmire.

Further extracts from *The History of the KSLI in the Great War 1914 -1918* note Eric's award of a mention in dispatches and while the second refers to the Gallant Shropshires' counter attack on April 21:

Herzeele. June 24, 1916 On June 24th the Brigade Commander, 16th Brigade inspected the battalion. Lieutenant (temp Captain) and Adjutant E G James was among those mentioned in Sir Douglas Haig's despatch of April 30th 1916.

St Omer. July 15, 1916 On July 1st the battalion left Herzeele and marched via Arneeke and Noordpeene to Tatinghem, two and a half miles west of St Omer to become training battalion for the Second Army Central School at Wisques. On 15th Lieutenant General Lord Cavan, XIV Corps Commander, inspected the battalion and again complimented them on their counter attack on April 21 saying that this operation had preserved the left flank of the army. After two years of war he declared he found everything in the battalion just as he wished it to be.

By the end of July 1916, Eric had been with the battalion in France for nineteen months – the first seven as a Rifle Platoon Commander and the last twelve as Adjutant. He had been Adjutant to the legendary Colonel Luard for eight months until he was mortally wounded in April. Since then he had been Adjutant to Colonel Bertie Murray, who also held Eric in high regard. As Adjutant during the last year in the Ypres Salient he had been the Commanding Officer's right hand man during all major operations, involving some bitter fighting in appalling conditions. During the last fourteen months the battalion had excelled itself and had gained high praise. But it had suffered heavy casualties – 188 killed, 765 wounded and 28 missing

Battle of the Somme

Two extracts from *The History of the KSLI in the Great War 1914–1918* describe the itinerary of the battalion's move from the Ypres Salient and redeployment in readiness to join the battle of the Somme. However, as Richard Holmes, the military historian observes the change of terrain from 'the dreary, drab and depressing surroundings of Flanders to the open plains of the Somme' which, being more akin to the rolling downs, fields and woods of southern England, must have lifted spirits.

On 1st August the battalion (40 officers and 873 other ranks) entrained at

18. Officers of the 1st Battalion KSLI in France in 1916. Eric as Adjutant, is seated on the right of his Commanding Officer, Lieutenant Colonel Bertie E. Murray DSO (seated middle of second row). [3]

Houpoutre for the Somme arriving at Douellens. After marching to camp at Englebelmer, they took over the trenches opposite Beaumont-Hamel on 15th August. They suffered a heavy bombardment on the 19th and again after their move to Auchonvillers on 25th when C Company's stretcher bearers received a direct hit. On 27th they were relieved in the trenches and marched to Naours, arriving on the 29th. On September 6th the battalion marched to Bois des Tailles, two miles east of Bray-sur-Somme arriving on the 8th and on the 11th took over trenches one mile from Maricourt.

Battle of Fleurs-Courcelette

On 14th September the battalion moved to trenches about 1,000 yards south west of Guillemont, preparatory to taking part in the general advance of the Fourth Army.

The battle of Fleurs-Courcelette, a sub-set of the Somme, is remembered for the debut of the tank and began on 15 September 1916. It was a multi-divisional push on a wide frontage to punch a gap in the German Third Position between the villages of Fleurs and Courcelette. Haig decided to set ambitious objectives for the Fourth Army so as to relaunch mobile operations and arrest the initiative from the Germans whose morale was considered suspect. However, the intensity of Royal Artillery support provided to the advancing troops was half that on 14 July and limited the successful outcome of the battle. This was because it had been decided to leave gaps in the barrage to avoid churning up the ground over which the

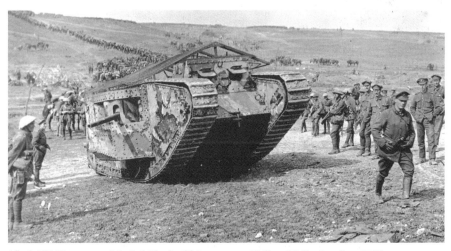

19. A 'C' Company Mark 1 Tank, Chimpanzee Valley 15 September 1916.

tanks would advance at 2 mph, too slow to keep up with advancing infantry. This meant that the weight of shells was insufficient to suppress the machine guns located in a major German strongpoint, known as the Quadrilateral, which was located in a tank lane. Of the fifteen tanks supposed to attack this strongpoint, only two took part in the fighting. Consequently these German machine guns were able to bring heavy fire to bear on both flanking divisions and cause heavy casualties among the troops of 6th Division advancing to the front of the Quadrilateral.

The History of the KSLI in the Great War 1914–1918 states:

The 6th Division was allotted the centre of the attack and advanced on a two Brigade front, 16th being on the right. The attack was made in three waves. First the 8th Bedfords were to take the first objective. Second the 1st Buffs were to pass through and take the second objective. Third the 2nd York & Lancaster Regiment supported by the KSLI were to pass through Morval village and establish a line north east of the village as a final objective.

The attack was launched at 6.20 am on 15th September. The 8th Bedfords were immediately held up by a strong point about 1,000 yards north east of the junction of Leuze and Bouleaux Woods, known as the Quadrilateral. The 1st Buffs went to assist but the second attack was no more successful. A third assault by 2nd York & Lancaster Regiment also

20. The 1st Battalion leaving the trenches near Ginchy in 1916 – a typical Western Front scene showing heavily laden soldiers crossing a devastated landscape.

failed. Shortly after midday the KSLI received orders to make a fourth assault on this formidable strongpoint from the south east, but these orders were cancelled during preparations for the attack, the 16th Brigade having suffered badly. The 18th Brigade made an unsuccessful attack on the Quadrilateral during the night of the 15/16th but by midday on the 16th the strongpoint remained in enemy hands.

Heavy artillery bombardment by our guns followed throughout the day including 12 inch guns. The Germans retaliated vigorously and an artillery duel lasted throughout the 17th.

It was during this that Eric was mortally wounded standing next to his Commanding Officer, Colonel Bertie Murray.

The loss of the Adjutant, Captain E G James, was a severe blow to the battalion. He had behaved with great gallantry during the 15/16th and received the DSO shortly before he died.

Despite the tactical shortcomings highlighted earlier and perceived with the benefit of hindsight, the British had taken the German Third Position on a front of 4,500 yards, and had advanced 2,500 yards. By the standards of 1916 the battle of Fleurs-Courcelette was a moderately successful set piece battle, which came at a high price.

As mentioned, Eric, who was known as Jimmy in the regiment, had shown outstanding gallantry on 15th September, the first day of the battle. Two days later he was mortally wounded in the head and finally succumbed to his wounds on 15th October. Family report has it that he was recommended for the Victoria Cross, but subsequent letters from his Commanding Officer, Lieutenant Colonel Bertie E Murray DSO and the Citation for his posthumous award of the Distinguished Service Order do not seem to substantiate this. However, his Commanding Officer's letters, while carefully worded to suit differing recipients, do give us a fair idea as to what happened.

Gallantry on 15 September 1916

Extract from the CO's letter to Mrs James dated 3 December 1916

'... on the afternoon of the 15th a stretcher and a carrying party were hit by a shell, and the wounded man was still alive although the others were dead. Jimmy wanted to go off and pick him up, but at the time I wouldn't let him as it was almost certain death. He would have gone, if it had been possible. Anyhow, a short time afterwards, I saw Eric and one of the men bringing the man back in a wheelbarrow.

I sent this action of his in when recommending him for the DSO, but it was not mentioned, although of course it probably helped him to get it, although he had earned it a good many times before.'

Citation

Second Lieutenant (temporary Captain) E G James, Shropshire LI

'For conspicuous gallantry during operations. He personally superintended with great skill all arrangements for two attacks on the enemy, and was dangerously wounded.'

Awarded on 19 November 1916 (posthumously)

Wounded on 17 September, 1916

Extract from the CO's letter to Mrs James dated 23 September 1916

'As you must know by now, he was wounded in the head on the 17th inst. The Padre who was with us took him to the best doctor in the Division (a Dublin specialist), who tells me that he has the greatest hope of his doing well, and we had him away within ten minutes of being hit.'

Extract from the CO's letter to Mrs Luard (wife of the former CO, the late Lieutenant Colonel Luard) dated 23 September 1916

'We were in action on 18th, 19th September and wiped the eyes of the Brigade, and succeeded in doing what every one else had failed to do. Casualties were light considering. Poor Jimmy was badly wounded the afternoon before, standing beside me; and there was I tearing my hair, with nobody to help me. It's added about ten years to my life ... The Battalion is still full of fight, which is the main thing however.'

Died of wounds on 15 October, 1916

Extract from the CO's letter to Mr James dated 26 October 1916

'I am more grieved than I can say to hear the sad news about Jimmy from Symonds-Taylor. We had not heard anything till yesterday, and I had hoped so much.

The only thing more I can say is that if ever a man deserved his DSO, Jimmy did, and that no man ever did more for this Battalion than he did. As an Adjutant he was perfect, tactful to a degree, and tireless in his work, and all the Battalion has done since he took over Adjutant is very largely due to him, and that is no small work. Although, of course your grief is great, I can assure you ours is little less.'

Somme in retrospect

There is precious little comfort for any family who lost someone in the battle of the Somme. During the Summer of 1916 over 1 million British, German and French soldiers died on the Somme. On 1 July alone – the British Army's bloodiest day – the appalling toll was nearly 60,000 killed, wounded, missing and taken prisoner. Of these 20,000 were killed.

An enthusiastic, but patchily trained British Army had believed that the 1st July was the start of the 'Big Push' to end the war. Instead it was the start of a bitter attritional struggle which ground on until the autumn, and was then followed by a further two years of bitter fighting. The sheer shock of so much death on the Somme for meagre territorial gain resonates today as strongly as ever and tends to numb the mind.

Until the 1980's the Somme continued to symbolise the wasteful, incompetent and futile fighting on the Western Front – a natural reaction for a nation in thrall to such a human tragedy. However latterly, due to painstaking and extensive studies by Military Historians, another view of the Somme has steadily emerged. Rather than being viewed in isolation, the battle is now taken in the context of the whole war. Germany occupied a huge swathe of Belgian and French territory in 1914. There was a clear logic in recovering this lost territory and relieving the hostage population. The German assault on Verdun in February 1916 lent a new urgency for the need for a British led offensive.

Military Historians now conclude that the Somme could not have been avoided, was strategically essential and transformed the British Army from a largely inexperienced mass army to a largely experienced one. It was forced to ascend a steep and agonising learning curve during which costly mistakes were made and opportunities missed. Charles Carrington, an infantry officer during the battle and author of *A Subaltern's War*, believed

21. Post Card: Hospital at Rouen in 1916.

that 'The British Army learnt its lesson the hard way, during the middle part of the Somme, and for the rest of the War, was the best Army in the field.' In short, the battle was not the complete failure of popular myth nor were the high command the *Donkeys* so cruelly portrayed. The coalition battle led by the British and ably supported by the French, relieved the pressure on the French at Verdun. It ground down the strength and morale of the German Army. Without the battle of the Somme, the Allies would never have won the 1st World War. This new retrospective provides comfort for the families of those Allied soldiers who lost their lives in this most costly of battles.

In Memoriam

Inside the book of letters so lovingly produced by his family, a practice much favoured by so many families at the time, there are two special letters which show so clearly the respect and affection in which Eric was held by everyone in the regiment.

The first was from Colour Sergeant H A Wallbank, who was Orderly Room Clerk from the time Eric became Adjutant in August 1915 until April 1916. Being posted to Base in April 1916 allowed Colour Sergeant Wallbank to pay regular visits to Eric in No 2 Red Cross Hospital in Rouen during late September and early October 1916. His pleasure, frustration and ultimate sadness are respectfully yet simply expressed.

Reg.Inf. Section No 3
G.H.Q., 3rd Echelon
20th October1916
Dear Sir,

> *I should like to let you know how sorry I was to hear of the death of your son, Capt. James, who died of wounds on 15th October. I was clerk to Captain James from the time he took over Adjutant in August 1915, to April this year, and know him pretty well, seeing each other day after day, and of course I came to know him fairly intimately. I, however, got a job at the Base in April, and so left the Battalion, but kept up my correspondence.*
>
> *I visited Captain James soon after he was admitted to Hospital at Rouen, and we had some talks. I had very little idea at those times that he was going to be taken, as he was so cheerful and smiled frequently. The last time I saw him he said he would like to see me again before he went to England, which he expected to do a few days later.*
>
> *The next time I called, I was told that he was desperately ill, and that his mother was with him. You can, perhaps, imagine the shock I received, expecting to find him improved. I went again the following two days, but was told his mother and brother were with him. Under the circumstances, I did not care to*

intrude, but I should dearly liked to have seen him once again. I asked a
Sergeant in the Inquiry Office at the Hospital to phone me if Captain James
had a change, but this was not done.
Not until the 19th October was I informed that Captain James had died. It was
too late, then, to even attend his funeral, and this grieved me further. I was
(as were all the officers and men) very fond of him, and shall never forget how
good he was to me. He gave me a splendid cigarette case when he returned from
leave, and this I shall always treasure as a memento of the best officer it has
been my lot to associate with. I served at the Front for 20 months, most of that
with Captain James. He was always so cheerful and brave, but was always
smiling. I am sure Colonel Murray will miss him terribly.
I lost my younger brother on the 28th of last month. Grief never comes singly.
I wish you would convey my sympathy to Mrs James. I hope you do not mind
my writing to you, but I could not be satisfied until I had done so.
Yours respectfully
H.A.Wallbank, Col.-Sergt.,
1st King's Shropshire L.I.

The second from Captain H S Collins DSO 1st Shropshires who was the
first man to be wounded in the war at Jogoland. Consequently he had to
write using his left hand.

From: Captain Collins DSO.
1st Shropshires
Lincoln Hill, Ross, Herefordshire
24th October 1916
Dear Mr James
I wish I could have got this letter off before seeing you, to let you know how
sorry I am for you and Mrs James on your great loss, and how greatly, like
everyone, I admired him.
Of all the many officers who have served with the regiment, I have always
considered Col. Luard, Col. Murray and your son the best. However bad the
times, they always seemed to be there, and Jimmy lasted longest of all. And
what I particularly admired about him was that, during the whole two years
of this miserable war he put in, he never once slacked off the smallest bit.
This would seem impossible, but with his stout heart he managed it.
From the day he joined he was always looked on as the most promising of the
officers, and, as an Adjutant, he was the best I ever knew, in peace or war. This
is paying a very high tribute indeed, as I have known a good many, and in
peace time adjutants were selected as being the best of captains and subalterns.
I know Col. Murray, who is the best soldier I know, was of the same opinion,

22. Eric's grave at St Sever Cemetery, Rouen.

and I can remember him saying once, when he thought Jimmy was going sick,
that he did not see how the regiment was going to get on without him.
He was easily the most popular of the offices; an Adjutant , if he does his job
properly, as he did, is bound to offend some people, but he was such a perfect
gentleman that no one ever resented anything from him. I know well how the
men loved him. No doubt we shall get a good Adjutant, but never another
Jimmy, – always tactful and cheerful, and, in difficult circumstances, the
bravest and coolest. Everyone will be sorry for you on the loss of such a
splendid son, and the Army has lost one of its best.
Yours sincerely
H.S.Collins.

For a twenty three year old, Eric had achieved so much – yet promised so
much more. To his family he was to become their Poppy in Foreign Fields.
Just one of a generation of outstanding young men cut down in their prime.

In the presence of many of his family, Eric was buried in Grave No 4801 at St Sever Cemetery, Rouen. By the Armistice in 1918 there were 12,000 British soldiers buried there.

On May 16 1918 his family presented two jewelled chalices to St Peter's Church, Hereford inscribed:

> To the Glory of God, and in loving memory of
> Captain Eric Gwynne-James DSO, 1st Bn KSLI,
> who died for his country, October 15, 1916
>
> *Non ille pro caris amicis*
> *Aut patria timidus perire**
>
> True love by life, – true love by death – is tried;
> Live thou for England – we for England died.

There is a Memorial inside the cloistered entrance to Cheltenham College Chapel to the 675 Old Cheltonians killed in the First World War. Eric's name is inscribed on one of the many brass plaques which adorn the nave of this beautiful Chapel. His name is engraved on the Family Memorial at Tupsley Church, Hereford.

On 4 November 1933 Eric's family attended a Dedication Service at St Chad's Church, Shrewsbury. The Roll of Honour bound within a Book of Remembrance lists the names of 4,752 men of the King's Shropshire Light Infantry who lost their lives in the Great War 1914 – 1918. This book lies in a beautifully carved oak cabinet within the vestibule of St Chad's Church. Each Sunday a page is turned. At this Dedication Service the Reverend Moore Darling gave an exceptional address, an extract of which is reproduced at Appendix 3.

During the mid 1970's, a few years after I left the army, we were visited by Lieutenant Colonel Bertie E Murray DSO, who was by then quite an old man. He and his wife had both decided that I should fall heir to some regimental silver which had been presented to them by the Officers of the KSLI as a wedding present on 30 June 1927. He seemed to remember Eric, his Adjutant of long ago, so vividly and with such enduring affection. My father and I both followed Eric into the KSLI and became Adjutant in 1935 and 1964 respectively. Colonel Bertie, who somehow seemed to bear the burden for Eric being killed, wanted to ensure that their pair of silver bugler statuettes and Shropshire LI helmet badges would find a suitable home.

---

* Not such as he was unready (reluctant or timid) to die for his dear friends or for his country.

23. The First World War Memorial in the Chapel Cloisters at Cheltenham College.

Appendices

Appendix 1   List of members of the James Family who have been
             educated at Cheltenham College.

Appendix 2   Eric's letter to Henry dated 17 February 1916.

Appendix 3   Extract from the Address given by The Rev Moore Darling
             at the Dedication Service of The Book of Remembrance
             containing The KSLI Roll of Honour of those killed in
             The Great War 1914–918 on 4 November 1933.

Appendix 1
Members of the Gwynne-James Family
who have been educated at Cheltenham College

Name	Year started at College	Remarks
Henry James	1841	Claimed to have been the first boy at College by mistaking the day when College first opened and arriving a day early. Later Lord James of Hereford. Died 1911.
Arthur Gwynne-James	1866	Later Sir Arthur Gwynne-James, Court Judge. Died 1936.
Francis Reginald James	1866	Solicitor, Gwynne-James & Sons. Died 1942.
Henry Percival James	1874	Solicitor in London. Died 1903.
Harold Gwynne-James	1905	Solicitor, Gwynne-James & Sons. Died 1964.
Eric Gwynne-James	1907	Captain Eric Gwynne-James DSO 1st Bn KSLI died of wounds sustained at the Somme in 1916.
Philip Gwynne-James	1913	Solicitor, Gwynne-James & Sons. Died 1980.
John Gwynne-James	1917	Brigadier John Gwynne-James DSO, formerly KSLI killed in action in Italy 1944.
David John Gwynne-James	1951	Captain in KSLI and later Ernst & Young.

24. Plaque in the nave of Cheltenham College Chapel

Appendix 2
Eric's letter to Henry dated 17 February 1916

AYLSTONE HILL,
HEREFORD.

Feb: 17ᵈ 1916.

My dear Henry.

I understand Mother has told you that I am home on leave. I came over on Sunday + have to return next Sunday. Very sorry you are not here as well. Mary + I go up to Brook St. tomorrow evening and we propose seeing "Bric-a-Brac" at the Palace + "Tonight's the Night" at the Gaiety on Saturday, as I hear both of these plays are excellent. My train leaves Victoria at 9.15 on Sunday morning.

Mary has been doing her 2ⁿᵈ Red X Exam this afternoon. I think she will sail through, as she appears to be full of knowledge about every kind of ailment from 'Plague' to "Housemaid's Knee". I lent her my head for an hour yesterday that she might practice bandaging scalp-wounds. The result was a huge success.

I ordered some books for you today. "The First Hundred Thousand" and "Carry On" by Ian Hay. I hear they are good but have not read them yet myself. Also "Fragments from France" by Capt. Bruce Bairnsfather. This is a collection of his pictures which have appeared weekly in the Bystander, and I think will amuse you greatly. I have told Rogers to send you some chocolates. Let me know if they don't arrive within the next fortnight.

Rumours are flitting about here that some of the Huns' ships nearly came out too far a few days ago. I believe there is some truth in it, but I expect you know

AYLSTONE HILL,
HEREFORD.

more about it than I do. Can't you entice them out? Try hanging some sausages from the masthead. 'Twould be a good riddance if they went for the bait.

Mary has just returned from her exam. She says she did not like the questions at all. But judging from the answers she gave, I am quite sure she has thwarted them very successfully.

We had some snow here yesterday so I am glad I was away from the jolly old ditch.

Let me know if you are hard up for cigarettes or anything at any time, or if you want any gadgets for your cabin —

Best of luck old man.

Yours affectly Eric.

25. Silver statuettes of KSLI Buglers and helmet badges, 85th King's Light Infantry.

Appendix 3

An Extract from the Address given by The Rev Moore Darling at the Dedication Service for the Book of Remembrance containing The KSLI Roll of Honour of those killed in The Great War 1914–1918.

The Hereford Times, Saturday 4 November 1933

War now only History The Rev Moore Darling took as his text the verse from Exodus 'A King arose in Egypt who knew not Joseph'.

He feared greatly, he said lest today there was growing up a generation that knew not Joseph; that could not get the hang of a service like this; that did not react to a service like this, because the War was only history, and not, as it was to him, humanity.

He suggested that there were two things the new generation had got to remember, 'War is Hell', he said, 'and if human wit can prevent it, it must never happen again. In War the nations of the world descend from civilisation into barbarism, put back the wheels of progress by a century'. But though war was hell, the late war brought out certain virtues, a certain nobility, a certain graciousness in human nature, that peacetime England was in danger of forgetting. There were three things conspicuous in that war which coming generations might well imitate. They were discipline, endurance and fellowship.

Discipline. We lived in an age when we were told the great thing was self expression, even if it stopped the other fellow expressing himself. We were told that we must let people develop. He had seen a tree develop so it pushed down a wall. 'No, there has to be discipline' he said. 'No one can be competent to order unless he has learnt to obey. I think one of the great things we have to learn today is to do what we are told'.

Endurance. Man would never achieve any mastery that mattered without endurance. It was the ultimate human virtue. He who could not take punishment would do little.

Finally, Fellowship – the cheapest word in the English language. People slapped each other on the back and parted in – fellowship. Fellowship was a stronger thing. It meant that we had been so thrown back on realities, we had so realised the futility of shams, we had found that common humanity was a bigger thing than class or creed. He did not believe fellowship could be built on any less foundation than that.

A *Generation Missing* 'Lastly' he went on, 'a generation of this country is missing. It is dead and buried. You and I have therefore got to do two man's work for England; our own and that of the man whose name is on that Roll of Honour outside. Unless we do his as well as our own, the job would not be done'. It meant that they and he were going out to be better Englishmen, better Christians, more and more determined while they got a living themselves, to care that the other fellow got a living too. That was about the best summary of Christianity he knew.

Family Recollections

None of the surviving members of the family were alive when Eric died on 15 October 1916. So, unlike his two younger brothers Henry and John, whom we do remember, we must rely on a mix of family anecdote and archive to outline the personality of a reputedly very special young man. Some photographs help to bring him into sharper focus.

Twelve years later in 1928, June was born and spent most of her early childhood in the family home at Aylestone Hill, Hereford while her parents Tina and Tony were stationed in India. During this time she inevitably absorbed family references to her Uncle Eric. Because Eric had been so dearly loved and had died so young, his brothers and sisters cherished and revered their memories of him. June's mother, Tina, who was six years younger than her brother Eric, had been a seventeen year old schoolgirl at St George's, Ascot when he died. Not surprisingly she fainted when she heard the news.

26. The Family Grave at Tupsley, Hereford.

My father John, aged thirteen when Eric died, had followed his older brother Eric to Moorland House Preparatory School in Heswall, Cheshire. It was a very bitter blow for him too. Extracts from three letters from the Headmaster, LJ Dobie to my grandfather during late October 1916 tell the story:

My Dear Mr and Mrs James
Dear Eric! – What a splendid example. I can just imagine his perfect patience and gentleness. I am so thankful that you both have been with him. But nothing can fully express the deep sympathy we feel for you.
John is so wonderful. He has just asked to be off for one day. So I have sent him to Nurse at Brightside.'
Dear John has been much closer to me all through this, and so gentle and brave. It has of course made a great impression upon him. Do you know out of the 1905 Cricket Eleven, in which Eric was, five have gone.

During Tina's long life she referred to Eric, as having set the standards for the family to emulate while her younger brother John, as being the greatest fun to be with. Consequently it is to June that we turn to as being best placed to pass on her impressions of an Uncle she never met.

Tina and Mary, the eldest of the eight children likened Eric to Chaucer's 'very gentle knight' because he was even tempered, generous and kind. He was apparently incapable of being cross with his mother, and to avoid fusses and rows he would retire to the lavatory.
The Arkwright family (Sir John Arkwright wrote the words to 'Oh Valiant Hearts') were devoted to him and I seem to remember that he was very fond of a lovely girl called Jean Bruce, who used to wear a man's cap. Apparently he was a natural horseman and he planned to farm in the Argentine after the first war ended.

When Eric was wounded at the Somme on 17 September 1916, and evacuated to No 2 Red Cross Hospital in Rouen.

'His father Frank, his mother Sophie, his sister Mary and his brother Harold travelled out to Rouen to be with him. By then it had become clear that if he survived he would have been a complete invalid. They knew he had died when the signet ring fell off his finger.

CHAPTER 3

Henry Gwynne-James
1896-1959

Early life

Henry, who was born on 12 May 1896, some three years after Eric, was the smallest of the eight children, yet his energy seemed to compensate for any lack of inches. Known within the family as Henny, he was much loved for his sense of fun. He took great pride in his family, relished being with his brothers and sisters, adored his father and mother and returned their love and affection with delight and generosity.

From a young age he was determined to join the Royal Navy. The discipline of a service existence and his devotion to his family soon became the pillars of his existence. Unlike Eric, Henry was of no more than average intellect but he applied himself diligently and energetically. His sporting activities, often hampered by his small stature and spare frame, owed more to enthusiasm than skill. However his natural zest for life and his relaxed spontaneous charm, skills honed from growing up in the hustle and bustle of a large family, gave him confidence socially. These innate and relaxed social skills were to stand him in good stead as his career progressed.

Royal Naval College Osborne 1909–1911 (aged 13–14)

On 15 January 1909 aged 13, Henry entered Osborne House, Isle of Wight as a Naval Cadet in the same term as Cadet HRH Prince Albert of Wales. Henry, together with seventy other thirteen year olds embarked on a life of rigid discipline and routine for a two year course designed to prepare them for life in the Senior Service. Osborne House was run by two key people, the Commanding Officer, Captain Christian, who was responsible for administration, discipline and naval instruction and also the Headmaster, Mr Godfrey, who presided over the broader aspects of education.

Each Cadet had a Tutor, a master who kept a record of his position and reports throughout his course. But the main influence on each Cadet was the Term Officer, an executive lieutenant of about twenty-six or twenty seven, chosen for his character and his technical or athletic abilities. It was the Term Officer who set the tone and moulded the characters of the cadets in his charge, awarding praise and blame where required; and it was he who organised games and dealt out punishments. In a way which does not usually happen in non-service schools, cadets modelled themselves, both consciously and instinctively on their Term Officers. Only six Term Officers had been selected from the wardrooms of the Royal Navy.

The Term Officer for the Grenville Term was Lieutenant William Phipps, whose character and temperament made him a natural and ideal example on which Cadets could model themselves. A splendid athlete and a strict disciplinarian Lieutenant Phipps had a perceptive understanding of human frailty. He could distinguish between the accomplished idler and the genuinely bewildered. To the first he was ruthless, to the second a friend in need. Prince Albert and his fellow Grenvilles keenly admired Lieutenant Phipps who clearly made a lifelong impression. When Albert became King in 1937, he appointed Captain William Duncan Phipps, CVO, RN (Retired) as his Gentleman-Usher-in-Ordinary.

Friendship with Prince Albert

By the summer of 1909 Henry will have learned most of the ropes at Osborne and in all probability was beginning to be well pleased at his choice of a career in the Royal Navy. His growing confidence and relaxed manner will have invited friendships many of which were to last throughout his life. Among this circle of friends was Prince Albert, who although popular did not make friends easily. In contrast to Henry, Prince Albert had a natural shyness and reserve in his human relationships, but once he made a friend he was a friend for ever. Henry, known as 'Jimmie' at Osborne, became one of Prince Albert's friends. This small circle included Colin Buist, George Cavendish, Bill Slayter and Miles Reid. Prince Albert continued to keep in touch with these friends long after he left the Navy and later became King. What appealed to his friends at Osborne was Prince Albert's 'sense of fun and mischief, his complete lack of side, his integrity and courage, and his general capacity for good fellowship'. He was, they all agreed, 'a fellow who would never let you down'.

As far as Henry was concerned, this friendship with Prince Albert and later the King was destined to last throughout their lives. This confidence was fiercely protected from the media and much cherished by Henry. He kept his many letters locked away and some twenty of these have been passed on to me. Sadly the Gieves storage depository in Bond Street, London where Henry had stored his belongings at the outbreak of the Second World War was bombed. It is probable that these belongings contained some others. However, for the interest of the reader I have reproduced those that I have inherited. They shed some light on a fine King in the making and an enduring friendship.

27. Prince Albert at RNC Dartmouth, 1912.

I reassure myself that I am not breaking my Uncle's confidence, as I also have correspondence between Henry and John Wheeler-Bennett, who in November 1952 was invited by the Royal Family to write a book on the personal and public life of King George VI. In 1958 John Wheeler-Bennett's book *King George VI. His Life and Times* was published by Macmillan & Co Ltd. This correspondence shows that under some pressure from the Author, Henry sent him these twenty letters on the condition that he did not mention Henry in his book. In his nine page cover letter dated 7 October 1953, Henry made comments and gave explanations on each letter to help the author understand who or what Prince Albert/King George VI was referring to. I have reproduced some of these comments and explanations for the reader's interest, as Notes to the letters. Now that fifty three years have elapsed since King George VI died in 1952, the Palace has kindly agreed to the publication of his letters to Henry.

Royal Naval College Dartmouth 1911–1912 (aged 15–16)

After successfully passing his entrance examination in December 1910, Henry entered RNC Dartmouth in January 1911. He and his 67 other former Grenvilles soon discovered that there was a world of difference between Osborne and Dartmouth. There was a sense of permanency and inherited tradition which Osborne lacked. After all the two sea veterans *Britannia* and *Hindoustan*, moored a little up river and still retained for technical instruction, had nurtured generations of naval cadets since 1863. However, by 1911, there were fine new College buildings set on a hillside overlooking the lowest reach of the River Dart.

Here, in this fine natural harbour, protected by the hills on either side and by the sudden bend in the river, cadets could get their first practical lessons in seamanship. First they learned to sail and pull small boats in sheltered waters before their training took them out to sea. All this demanded a greater manliness and sense of responsibility for in less than three years they would become midshipmen in His Majesty's Royal Navy. At the same time there were greater freedoms and opportunities to enjoy one of the most beautiful spots in England. Yet the start of the spring term was plagued by a great epidemic of measles which swept throughout England. This was a particularly virulent and persistent form of the disease which could be re-contracted up to three times. At one moment more than two thirds of the cadets were in the sick-bay simultaneously, of whom two were to die during the epidemic. When the Prince of Wales and Prince Albert contracted the disease – in both cases quite severely – bulletins were issued to the Press.

Various events during this two year period caught the imagination of the Cadets. One was the coronation of King George V, followed by a mighty gathering of warships at Spithead in June 1911. Others would have been Captain Scott's expedition to the Antarctic and the disastrous sinking of SS *Titanic*.

The Grenvilles proved to be a spirited group and there was a good deal of 'skylarking' at Dartmouth at the time. Two such incidents included putting out all the lights on the Quarter deck during a Saturday night dance and introducing a flock of sheep, supplemented by a quantity of cocks and hens, during the ensuing darkness. However, as the terms sped by Henry, like his fellow Grenvilles, were already excited at the prospect of the final training cruise in foreign waters. On successful completion the cadets would qualify for the dirk and patches of a midshipman. This seven month cruise, a further stage in the progressive preliminary training of a naval officer, was to be aboard the 9,800-ton *Cumberland* due to sail from Devonport on January 17, 1913. Prince Albert wrote to Henry during their Christmas leave:

York Cottage (to Aylestone Hill, Hereford)
Sandringham, Norfolk
December 26th 1912
Dear James

   Many thanks for your letter. I am very glad you appreciate the photograph I gave you. I hope you are having a decent leave. I suppose you are coming up to London to go down by the special train to Devonport on the 17th of next month. If so, will you let me know because then we could make arrangements to go down together as we did to Dartmouth once. My father told me the other day that he had heard from the Admiralty that I had passed out.[4] The official list has not yet come out. Cooper is coming with us in the Cumberland after all. I am very pleased, aren't you? He is such a nice man and knows our term so well. Wishing you a very happy New Year
   I remain
   Yours very sincerely
   Albert

January 18–July 8 1913. HMS Cumberland
Armoured Cruiser. Training Cruise. Aged 17
(displacement tonnage 9,800; overall length x breadth 440 x 66 ft; armament fourteen 6 in, nine 12 pdr; London & Glasgow 16.12.1903)
Itinerary: Tenerife–St Lucia–Trinidad–Barbados–Martinique–San Domingo–Puerto Rico –Jamaica–Havana–Bermuda–Halifax– Quebec– Gaspe–St John's Newfoundland–Plymouth.

Because of Prince Albert's presence on the cruise the Press took a close interest in proceedings as evidenced by an extract from *The Observer* dated 19 January 1913.

Prince Albert's Voyage.

The Cumberland leaves for the Canaries.

With Prince Albert, Their Majesties' second son on board, the cruiser *Cumberland* left Devonport yesterday afternoon for the Canary Islands and a three month's cruise in the West Indies, to be followed by about two months in the Mediterranean.[5]

His Royal Highness joined the cadet cruiser with 66 other cadets on Friday afternoon. He was not officially received, and, indeed, no distinction was made between him and other cadets, except that this morning the Commander-in-Chief, Admiral Sir William May, visited the *Cumberland* and had a brief conversation with the young Prince.

Prince Albert took leave of his parents on Thursday, and on Friday he left London for Plymouth. In the same train there were fifty or sixty cadets. He received a cordial welcome from his colleagues. On his arrival at Plymouth he was recognised by a few people who had previously seen the Prince of Wales.

Prince Albert bears a great facial resemblance to his older brother. No formality whatever was observed; nobody was at the station to meet the Prince, except a warrant officer (Mr William A Hearn, Gunner), who was sent from the *Cumberland* to conduct the cadets to the ship. The Prince took his bags from the compartment and placed them on the platform, and when he had seen that they were taken care of by one of the working party sent from the ship, he walked to the brake waiting outside the station.

The Prince laughed good humouredly at the journalists, photographers and the few people about eager to catch a view of him. When the photographers had snapped him he told them to have a go at some of the others.

Captain Aubrey Smith received the cadets on board according to seniority, and the Royal cadet slept Friday night in a hammock in the cadets' quarters.

At Osborne and Dartmouth cadets had received a good grounding in physics and mathematics and had become familiar with various types of engines and other mechanical devices used by ships of war. They had acquired a fair knowledge of essential subjects for a naval officer. This cruise translated theory into practice, from classroom and workshop to the quarter-deck and engine-room platform of a modern man-o'-war. They saw in a wider sphere how obedience, responsibility and practical knowledge of tasks melded together in those they were destined to command. The cadets coaled ship and stood their watches under the supervision of their officers. They also pursued their technical and academic studies in classes. All this was set against the inestimable advantage of what for many was their first contact with the world outside. From a general horizon bounded by the playing fields of the Royal Naval College they were visiting foreign climes and meeting strange peoples. It gave some idea of the vastness of that far flung Empire, which in due course they would be called upon to serve and defend.

As HMS *Cumberland* steamed towards Tenerife, Henry was soon to experience sea sickness induced by the renowned steady role of the Bay of Biscay. Fortunately he was in good company, for most of the cadets, including Prince Albert, and some officers also succumbed. However, it must have been unpleasant to discover that he was a poor sailor – an affliction destined to dog his future career.

Naturally the presence of Prince Albert, who was to be treated like any other cadet, invited much interest when HMS *Cumberland* docked at all ports on the itinerary. Indeed at Trinidad, Barbados, Jamaica and Bermuda demonstrations and enthusiasm were immense. As he stood to speak in Jamaica a cluster of young ladies had an overriding ambition to touch the trousers of the White Prince. As he spoke they prodded his ankles and thighs in an excess of loyal admiration, one was overheard to whisper to another: 'Say, have you touched the Prince?' to which her friend replied ecstatically, 'Yes, three times'.

Slowly the cruise ran its course as *Cumberland* passed from the tropical charms of the Caribbean to the more rugged scenery of Canadian waters. The size of the Canadian lakes and the immense distance covered by water into the heart of the country impressed the cadets. A fascinating day of tourist interest began at Toronto at seven in the morning and ended at Quebec twelve hours later, during which the cadets visited Niagra Falls, sailed through the lovely scenery of the Thousand Isles and shot the rapids at Long Salt. Social functions and various balls followed at Quebec. On the Gaspe peninsula and in Newfoundland there was salmon fishing. There was one alarming moment off the Canadian coast when *Cumberland* ran into a considerable storm. A large wave coming aboard caught Prince Albert and one or two others and sucked them to the side of the ship. An onlooker said 'He was as near as toucher washed overboard'.

Cumberland returned to her home port of Plymouth on July 8 1913, and the cadets were granted a week's home leave before completing the remainder of the training period on manoeuvres off the Nore. Henry and his fellow cadets were to be appointed Midshipmen on September 15 1913.

The Midshipman has now disappeared from the sea-going Navy, but in his time the 'snotty' was regarded as 'the lowest form of marine life'. He was subject to a very rigid discipline at the hand of his superiors, being at their beck and call, rather in the manner of a 'fag' at a public school. When off duty, his world was the Gunroom, where his superior was the junior Sub-Lieutenant, who exercised his autocratic powers according to his own character, sometimes as a benevolent despot and sometimes as a bloody tyrant. Moreover, the Midshipman enjoyed no sense of privacy. On the flat outside the Gunroom, which he shared with a dozen others or more, his clothes and personal belongings were stored in his sea-chest and above this he slung his hammock at night and stowed it a way in the morning. There was nowhere he could be alone – a considerable privation when one is seventeen. His duties included standing watch, taking his picket-boat from ship to shore, labouring in the pitch black hold of a dirty collier in the gruelling work of coaling ship, and finishing up with the traditional meal of bread and cheese, onions and beer before turning in.

28. Henry as a Midshipman with his mother outside Aylestone Hill.

During August Henry received a flurry of letters from Prince Albert and from the Admiralty regarding his posting HMS *Collingwood*:

HM Yacht Victoria & Albert
6 August 1913
Dear Jimmie
> *... We are joining the Collingwood at the end of September, and in February we go to the Mediterranean, but for how long I do not know. Well that is something and I will let you know any further developments.*
> *The weather here has been lovely for racing and on Monday my father won a race in the Britannia. She sailed beautifully and left the others standing.*
> *I hope you will have a good leave and that the weather will be fine. Well so long.*
> *Yours very sincerely*
> *Albert*

Balmoral Castle
15 August 1913
Dear Jimmie
> *I am enclosing to you the photographs which you wanted and they arrived the day before yesterday. I am very glad to be up here again as the air is so invigorating. I arrived here last night with my mother. I have not heard anything more about the Collingwood. I do not know whether I told you before but I shall very likely join her at Queensferry. What fools those people were, who went off at Cowes smoking on the boat to Portsmouth. They must have been mad*[6]*.*
> *Well so long.*
> *Yours sincerely*
> *Albert*

Admiralty to Mr PHG James RN
c/o FR James, Aylestone Hill, Hereford
28th August 1913
Percival HG James
> *The Lords Commissioners of the Admiralty hereby appoint you Midshipman of His Majesty's Ship Collingwood and direct you to repair on board that ship. Your appointment is to take place from the 15th September 1913.*
> *You are to acknowledge the receipt of this appointment forthwith, addressing your letter to the Commanding Officer, HMS Collingwood taking care to furnish your address and asking instructions as to joining.*
> *By Command of their Lordships,*
> *Admiralty*

Balmoral Castle
31 August 1913
Dear Jimmie

> *I received my appointment to the Collingwood yesterday. I saw the others who were appointed in the papers. But Jack Briggs⁷ was not in the list of names for the Collingwood. He has been appointed to the Princess Royal. It is very bad luck on him and us, as he is such a nice chap and I thought that he would have certainly got the Collingwood. I have written to Jack about it. ...*
> *Yours very sincerely*
> *Albert*

HMS Collingwood
3 September 1913
Midshipman James

> *You are to join HMS Collingwood at Queensferry by 7pm (at the latest) on 27th September 1913. A boat will leave Hoare's Pier, South Queensferry at 7.0pm on that day. In the event of your arriving earlier you are to inform me of the time of arrival at South Queensferry, addressing your letter or telegram to the Commanding Officer HMS Collingwood, c/o GPO London.*
> *James Ley*
> *Captain*

Balmoral Castle
11 September 1913
Dear Jimmie

> *Many thanks for your letter. ...*
> *I am joining the Collingwood at Queensferry on the 29th.*
> *The stalking season here has been very bad. We have only killed 24 stags, while last year at this time we killed 41, just about double. The weather has been much too warm and dry, and therefore they are in great droves and it is impossible to get near them. I have had three blank days running.*
> *I hope your wireless will be a success. My brother arrived here on the 6th and is very pleased to be back in England again. He was fed up with Germany. Hoping you are having a decent time.*
> *Yours very sincerely*
> *Albert*

Although there is no written evidence to support this, it gradually became apparent to Henry that he was expected to keep a friendly eye on Prince Albert. Being friends since Osborne days this will have been both an honour and a pleasure.

1913–1916. HMS *Collingwood*

Battleship. Aged 17–19

(displacement tonnage 19,250; overall length x breadth 500 x 84 ft;
armament ten 12 in; twenty 4 in; Devonport Dockyard 7.11.1908)

When the Midshipmen joined HMS *Collingwood* in September 1913, the battleship was flying the flag of Vice-Admiral Sir Stanley Colville, commanding the First Battle Squadron of the Home Fleet. Admiral Colville was an old friend and former shipmate of King George, but this made no difference to the status of the newly appointed Midshipman Prince Albert, known as Mr Johnson, who like Henry and other fellow Grenvilles were 'the lowest form of marine life'.

The First Battle Squadron sailed from Devonport on 28 October 1913 to join manoeuvres in the Mediterranean, and later to cruise in Egyptian and Aegean waters. Being part of a fleet-in-being and witnessing British naval sea-power on manoeuvres for the first time must have been awesome. The Fleet then sailed to Alexandria, Athens, Naples and Toulon before returning to Gibraltar where HMS *Collingwood* spent a fine warm Christmas Day at anchor in the harbour, before returning to Devonport in time to spend New Year's eve at home in England. Henry could reflect on an eventful year. As a seventeen-year old he had journeyed 13,000 miles and had seen more of the world than many see in a lifetime. Small wonder that his younger brother, John, aged 10 was impressed and decided to follow Henry into the Royal Navy.

In early January 1914, while home in Hereford on leave, Henry received a brief note and photograph from Prince Albert:

Buckingham Palace
December 31st 1913
Dear Jimmie
    I am sending you the photograph I promised you. I hope you arrived safely
    at home yesterday, and that you will have a really good leave.
    Wishing you the best of luck in the coming year.
    I remain
    Yours very sincerely
    Albert

The next six months of normal service in *Collingwood* with First Battle Squadron included a tour up the west coast of Scotland, during which the Prince of Wales was the guest of the ships captain, Captain Ley. Henry will have met 'Mr Johnson's' older brother. Later while *Collingwood* was at Portland on 28 June 1914 news came of the assassination of the Archduke Franz Ferdinand at Sarajevo. The Archduke had been King George's guest at

PRINCE ALBERT.

29. Below: HMS *Collingwood*.
30. Right: Prince Albert by 12 in Gun HMS *Collingwood*, 1913.

Windsor only six months before. However, it is doubtful if most Englishmen would have had any idea of the repercussions of this incident in the Balkans.

Fortunately the British Cabinet, on the initiative of Mr Churchill, had decided the previous summer to hold a Test Mobilisation of the Fleet in July 1914. The Naval Reserve, though not legally liable, had been invited to join their ships and upwards of 20,000 reservists reported to their depots. On July 20 this great armada, including *Collingwood*, put to sea for exercises of various kinds. At Spithead it took more than six hours for eighteen miles of warships running at high speed to pass before King George V, aboard *Victoria and Albert*.

As the threat of war intensified, so on 26 July all leave was cancelled and, despite the allotted time for reservists having expired, the First Sea Lord, Prince Louis of Battenberg, issued an order to retain the Fleet in a state of preparedness for war. Two days later Austria declared war on Serbia while the British Fleet steamed from Portland to concentrate with all speed and secrecy at Scapa Flow. In *Collingwood*, Henry and the rest of the fore Turret 'A' Team periodically adopted war stations and performed their duties as watchkeepers, control officers and searchlight officers. There must have been a new urgency in their actions and much excitement as to what lay ahead. At 2am on 4 August war was declared on Germany.

First World War

Within three weeks of the outbreak of war Prince Albert, much to his frustration, went down with appendicitis and a few days later part of the Grand Fleet experienced their first formal naval action. Henry will have been dismayed to see 'Mr Johnson' evacuated from *Collingwood* to the hospital ship *Rohilla* and then to hear that he had been admitted to the Northern Nursing Home in Aberdeen. Henry will also have been disappointed that *Collingwood* was not involved in the battle of Heligoland Bight, when Admiral Sir John Jellicoe in *Iron Duke* led the other part of the fleet to the first naval victory of the war, sinking three German cruisers and two destroyers.

It turned out that Prince Albert's appendicitis was serious. It was not until after a prolonged convalescence and a subsequent shore posting on the War Staff at the Admiralty, that he was finally declared fit to return to HMS *Collingwood* at Portsmouth on 12 February 1915, after an absence of nearly six months. During this period Henry received a letter from a Prince who clearly felt that nineteen was no age to be 'on the beach' while the flower of England, which included many of his friends, were being decimated at Ypres and La Bassée. This letter shows his longing to return to duty and a genuine concern for his colleagues, both traits later destined to exemplify his reign as King.

York Cottage, Sandringham
Norfolk
30th October 1914
Dear Old Jimmie

I hope you will not be surprised at me not having written to you before, but I have been very busy in London, and have not had much time to myself. I hope you are well and flourishing, and not too tired of waiting.

As you may imagine I was terribly cut up about leaving the Collingwood with that bloody appendicitis. Thank God I am all right again, and am eagerly waiting the time when I can return to duty. I have been on leave now for 3 weeks, and the latest that I have heard from the doctors is that it will be 3 months before I can get back. Old Treves, the surgeon I expect you have heard of, is quite ancient as regards appendicitis, and I hope to get back in about 3 weeks from now. If I am not allowed to I shall fret till I am allowed. I am feeling ever so much better than I ever did before. It seems odd that the fleet have done nothing since I left on August 23rd, just two months ago. Everything seems to be going on very well at the front, and the monitors have done splendidly and smashed up some of their big guns. I wonder what you think about Prince Louis's resignation as 1st Sea Lord, and Fisher taking his place. Personally I think it most unfair as he has devoted his whole life to the Navy, and is such an able man.

I have had several days shooting since I have been here. We arrived today for the weekend and are going to have two day's shooting. My father is terribly tired with all his work and is only too thankful to get down here for a rest. I hope you have plenty of warm clothes etc. I have just got heaps of things from old Gieve. Leather waistcoats, fur lined sou'westers and a leather coat to wear under the greatcoat. Do let me know if there is anything you want, such as cigarettes or books or something. For the former what sort have you got in the gunroom, because I propose to bring up that sort so as not to be short of them during the month. As your letters are read just put a 1 for De Reszhe, and a 2 for Pera, and then I shall understand which you have got. I can always send some up to you if you are getting short.

Life in London is very dull now, and everything terribly dark.

Will you please ask Talbot[8] whether he sent the things I told him to. In case he never got the letter I will tell you what they are:

All dirty washing
Greatcoat
Pair of nailed shoes

I hope everybody is very well on board and please remember me to all the gunroom. How are the new snotties getting on? You must be pleased to have

somebody to do the dirty work. Tait[8] writes to me occasionally and tells me how
you are getting on. By the way are you in want of any cocoa? I could get some
sent up for the use of the gunroom if Philpotts[8] can't get any sent.
Well so long my dear old thing and I will write again if anything of interest
happens.
I feel such a shit here, doing nothing when I ought to be with you,
The very best of luck
Yours very sincerely
Albert

As *Collingwood* played her part in patrolling the coasts of Britain, so Henry
and his shipmates now experienced the monotonies and strain of long
periods of watch and ward at sea. Occasional brief snatches of shore leave at
Rosyth were welcome. By the turn of the year the routine changed to units
of the Fleet going out into the North Sea for three days at a time and remaining in Scapa Flow for ten. The monotony of the three days' patrolling at sea
was relieved by moments of vivid excitement when any contact was made
with the enemy.

The welcome return of Prince Albert to the *Collingwood* was sadly short-
lived as three months later his gastric troubles returned and in early July
1915 once again he was compelled to leave the *Collingwood*. Then under the
supervision of a new doctor he made a very slow but steady recovery, but it
was not until May 5 1916 – ten months later – that the doctors finally agreed
that he was fit to return to the *Collingwood*. During this period he wrote a
Christmas card and three letters to Henry.

Henry, now a senior Midshipman, no longer kept watch at sea, but
alternated between being in control of searchlights by night and in charge of
submarine look-outs by day. In harbour he worked as an assistant to the
Gunnery and Torpedo Lieutenants and ran the steam pinnaces and picket-
boats under the supervision of the Commander. For recreation there was
gymnastics and boat pulling exercises, the latter being a test for Henry's
small frame. Ashore there was football and hockey, but little else.

York Cottage
Sandringham
Norfolk
24th December 1915

   It does seem ages since we last saw each other. I am sending you a box of
   chocolates, which I hope you will like. I am longing to get back again to the
   ship as I am now quite well. I hope you are just as hearty as ever and very
   well. That bit of leave must have been a Godsend to you.

My father has quite recovered from his accident [9] *now, and hopes to shoot*
next week.
Ever
Yours very sincerely
Albert

The next letter, addressed to Sub-Lieutenant PHG James RN, HMS
Collingwood, 1st Battle Squadron c/o GPO, describes his four day visit to the
Prince of Wales at the Headquarters of the Guards' Division at La Gorgue at
the end of January 1916.

Buckingham Palace
16 February 1916
My dear old Jimmy
　　Very many thanks for your two letters. So sorry not to have answered the first
　　one before but I have been so busy with my work at the Admiralty and here. I
　　go there twice a week and Avery [10] *the NO who was in the 'Cumberland' works*
　　with me also twice a month. I don't have much time to myself which is a good
　　thing, as it makes the time go faster and I can't return to the ship till April at
　　the earliest. It is a nuisance as the time seems to get put off every time the
　　doctors see me and I feel perfectly well.
　　I had a very good 4 days in France with my brother at the beginning of the
　　month. I went with him to La Gorgue, the HQs of the Guards Division. I saw
　　a great deal but did not actually go into the front line trenches as I was not
　　allowed to. Utter 'balls', but still I suppose someone would have had to take the
　　responsibility if I had been 'sniped'. As it was I saw several houses shelled by
　　the Bosches and women and children running out by the back doors. That
　　makes one think of the horrors of the war and those people are shelled every
　　day. They won't leave the houses as they have nowhere to go to. They have got
　　quite accustomed to it by now. One morning I went to breakfast in a 'dug-out'
　　which has been built inside a ruined farm 400 yds from the trenches. It is the
　　battalion HQs when they are in the trenches.
　　The next day I went to Kemmel a hill in Belgium and it is used as an Artillery
　　Observation Post and I got a good view of Ypres and the surrounding country.
　　Most of our guns there were shelling the enemy trenches and a town just
　　behind their lines. I watched a 12in howitzer fire.
　　The day when I saw the houses being shelled was near Béthune further south of
　　La Gorgue. We went up Foise No 9, a slag heap and saw Loos, Hulluch, La
　　Bassée etc, all the country near the fighting in September 1915. My brother
　　lived in Béthune during July till September, so he knew all the places well.
　　Everyone out there seemed very cheery but their life is very much rougher than

ours in the Fleet. I heard the other day that the German Fleet was coming out
sooner than we expected. There are various reports that Germany has no more
food and that they are also having food riots. But this seems to occur in towns
far from Berlin. Personally I don't believe anything I read in the papers.
I regularly hear from Tait[10] and he tells me what news there is. But I like
getting your letters as I never see anybody in the Fleet so never hear any news
from that quarter. I dined with Sir S Colville[10] last night and he told me several
things I did not know about. He had a very good week in France and went into
the trenches and fired every kind of gun and rifle and grenade. He was nearly
'sniped' once, which of course pleased him greatly. He is very sick about
Portsmouth, but it is better than the Admiralty.
I am afraid that this is about all the news now. I will write again shortly and
tell you some more. I suppose the gramophone is still going strong. I have just
got one for my sister. It helps to pass the time. Have you got the 'Bric-a-Brac'
revue records? Their songs are very good and you ought to get them if you have
not got them already. I know them all by heart. Let me know if you want them.
Hoping you and Cavendish[10] are both very well and pleased with the cabin.
Ever
Yours very sincerely
Albert

During March 1916 Henry, then nearly 20, had a three week appointment as
No 1 of HMS *Foxglove*, a Flower Class Minesweeper, which must have been
an exciting and welcome break after two and a half years with the
Collingwood. Such a long period with one ship, which ultimately spanned
nearly three and a half years, was unusual and supports the theory that
Henry had been posted to the *Collingwood* as he was considered to be
suitable to keep a friendly eye on Prince Albert. Because of this confidential
arrangement, of which Henry may not have been fully aware, Prince
Albert's two periods of illness, totalling 16 months, had the effect of
prolonging Henry's tour of duty in the *Collingwood* pending Prince Albert's
return to duty. This had the effect of delaying Henry's next appointment.
Prince Albert's next letter to Henry recounts, in an engaging way, how he
discovers that his suspicions are correct and typically considers taking steps
to remedy the situation for his friend.

Buckingham Palace
19 March 1916
My Dear James
    Very many thanks for your letter. You must have been glad to have got away
    from the old Collingwood for a few days. It must make a change and being

No 1 of the Foxglove must be more exciting than the other job.

As a matter of fact 'arry Tait told me all about your other confidential job[11] but he only treated it as a joke. He also said that Jimmy[11] has promised you something good in the future, I think I know what his reasons were for not letting you go. He has got some idea in his head that you can't leave the ship without my father's permission, as he had you specially appointed there when we first went to sea. This question has cropped up several times, the first being when Turnour[11] left for that flying job. When Tait came on leave I had a long talk with him about it, and he thought it best to leave it for the present. Before I return I am going to talk the matter over with my father and get to the bottom of it once and for all. I am certain he will understand what Jimmy means and will give orders for it to be cancelled. I know what bad luck it is on you, but you know as well as I do what Jimmy is on a matter like that, and won't do anything till it is down on paper. I told Cavendish all this when I last saw him so he also knows the reason for his not having left.

I saw Captain Brand, the 2nd Sea Lord's Assistant and he told me that as soon as I got back something might change. I hear that you are taking over the Gunroom when Christie[11] gets promoted – at least I suppose he is promoted now, as he ought to have been on the 15th.

Of course all this won't go any further than me, but I thought I should like to tell you exactly how things are. Tait often spoke to me about this in the ship so it is quite all right as he never repeats anything. You need not tell him that I have told you all this or mention the fact that I am going to ask my father. He writes to me regularly and tells me all the little interesting things that happen on board. I think it will be all right returning next month.

This life here is getting intolerable. You don't know what it is like to have to live in this sort of prison. It is a great trial when asking to go out in the evening, as they (my parents) always want to know exactly what you're going to do, and even go as far as asking what you are going to eat at dinner! This last is the limit, but it is no good giving in so I do get out about twice a week which is always something. I must leave here soon as things are getting too hot for me, always having to tell the most awful lies and it won't be long before I get caught out. I am becoming an expert liar so when we do meet again you must not mind if I tell you some cawkers till I lose the habit.

I have been playing squash with Greig[11] lately. He is in the 'Attentive' at Dunkerque and has been on leave for a bit. Just the same as ever merry and bright as he always was. You know he's been married, and I met her the other day. I have also seen Percy who is on sick leave with dysentery! Also very much the same, and his laugh quite the same. I have also got heaps to tell you on every kind of subject.

I see there is a man named Hampden at the Admiralty. What he does I don't

know but I will try and find out for you. Well I must be stopping now and I
hope this will ease your mind on the subject in question. Not a word to anyone.
The best of luck to you.
Ever
Yours very sincerely
Albert

Henry completed his three week attachment to HMS *Foxglove* and returned
to the *Collingwood* on 26 March 1916 to take over the Gunroom. A few days
later he received a letter from Prince Albert giving notice of his return.

Buckingham Palace
27th March 1916
My Dear James

Very many thanks for you letter. I am so glad you found my letter a relief and
of course I will remember about you if I ever get a chance of getting somebody
a job, when there is one going. Nothing doing at the present I think, and the
Admiralty is the last place where one hears of anything. I have found out that
Hampden has just gone over to America and won't be back till the end of April.
I don't know whether this will help to solve the mystery of the secret job, but
I expect it may. Did you know the man or did he just write and ask you if you
would like to go?

Tait told me that I was going to have Marsh's old cabin which I understand is
vacant. The one next to Christie's. By the way, has he been promoted? I expect to
be back any time after the 12th of April. That is when Bertrand Dawson[12]*comes*
over here from France so I hope to see him then. I think he ought to let me.

Last week my father and mother gave three days entertainments here for
wounded sailors and soldiers outside London. Everything went off very well
and it was a great success. It made a change in the routine of life.

Well hoping to be back again in a month's time.
Ever
Yours very sincerely
Albert

As recorded in his next letter dated 20 December, Prince Albert's concern
that his ten months' sick leave had delayed Henry's next posting proved to
be well founded. However, this delay turned out to be fortuitous from
Henry's point of view, while the Prince's return to the *Collingwood* at Scapa
Flow on 5 May was timely. Within fourteen days of their promotion to Sub
Lieutenant on 15 May 1916, both young men were to experience their first
battle at sea.

Battle of Jutland

During the Spring of 1916, there had been signs in Germany that the High Seas Fleet needed to justify its existence in the eyes of the German people. Their Army's appalling sacrifices at Verdun[13] and the increasing severity of the British blockade demanded retaliatory action.

Germany's Admiral von Scheer's offensive plan was to use his battle-cruisers to bombard Sunderland and to tempt Sir David Beatty to come out from his base at Rosyth to be destroyed by U-boats lying in wait. By coincidence, Sir John Jellicoe's own plan was to force von Scheer to do just this. In the event, inclement weather prevented either plan from being put into effect. Von Scheer, who depended on aerial reconnaissance by Zeppelins to protect his battle cruisers from being caught unawares, could not proceed as bad weather prevented the flying of Zeppelins.

While his U-boats waited in vain at their rendezvous for the weather to clear, von Scheer knew he could not delay his offensive beyond 30 May, as soon afterwards they would then have to return to base. When the weather refused to clear he ordered the battle cruisers to proceed to the Skagerrak, ensuring that their presence off the Norwegian coast became known to the British Admiralty. This had the desired effect and on the night of 30 May the British Fleet from Scapa and Cromarty under Sir John Jellicoe and the fast fighting squadrons from Rosyth under Sir David Beatty put to sea. The scene was set for the greatest naval battle of the war.

Much has been written about this great Battle of the Mists, but it is not for a biographer, with no knowledge of naval strategy and tactics to describe such a battle. Much less to offer an opinion and enter into the disputes and controversy which later ensued as to its conduct. However, in purely statistical terms the British Navy lost 14 ships and the German Navy 11 ships. In capital terms the Royal Navy lost 3 battle cruisers to 1 German. Hence overall the Battle of Jutland was perceived as a slight German tactical victory. British cruisers were found to have thin skins while our inferior shells were deflected by German thicker armour, despite striking their target.

Instead let us concentrate on Henry's 'Turret A' (Twin 12 inch) team under command of Lieutenant Tait in the *Collingwood*. Prince Albert was the Second in Command. There are five entries of interest in the Ships Log:

6/5/1916	7.30 am HRH Prince Albert rejoined ship. Scapa Flow.
16/5/1916	Weighed anchor Scapa Flow.
31/5/1916	4 pm Hands to Action Stations. 56 degrees 52 minutes North (latitude), 5 degrees 42 minutes East (longitude).
	6.40 pm Engaged enemy's Battle Cruisers, Light Cruisers and

Destroyers at long range. Observed damage to HMS *Marlborough*.
Observed serious damage to a ship of Shannon or Warrior Class.
Observed damage to *Seydlitz* and a ship of Augsberg Class.
9.15 pm Hands to Night Defence Stations.

1/6/1916   2.20 am Action stations.

3.45 am Sighted enemy Schultz-Lang airship steering north.

2.20 pm 16 knots. Commenced zig zagging every 15 minutes.

22/6/1916   A Turret to loading drill.

Ships Logs are essentially brief and factual as to location etc but do not give much away. When being called to Action Stations on 31 May, it became clear that the *Collingwood* was under heavy attack from torpedo craft, but those on board saw little more of the main German battle fleet than the distant orange flashes of their guns. But they did see other evidence of the carnage of battle. They passed the wreck of the *Invincible*, the flagship of the Second Battle Cruiser Squadron; they watched the tragedy which overwhelmed Sir Robert Arbuthnot's cruiser squadron when, caught between two fleets, enveloped in a shifting cloud of smoke, spray and bursting shells, they seemed to fall to pieces as if bashed by a gigantic hammer. Unable to do anything but watch – for the enemy was still hidden – they saw first *Defence* and then *Black Prince* disappear beneath a pall of spray and smoke.

Their turn came when *Derfflinger* suddenly loomed up in the mist, leading a division of the enemy and deploying into line, and into this enormous target they fired three salvos at 8,000 yards' range with great effect. Through their glasses they could see huge holes torn in the enemy's side, exposing the main deck which glowed like a furnace, with flames leaping up through a rent in the quarter-deck. They could not administer the final *coup de grace* before their quarry turned away to be hidden in the rolling mists. *It was nine o'clock by now and nearly dusk,* as Prince Albert wrote to his brother, the Prince of Wales. *We packed up for the night and manned the 4in guns for repelling destroyer attacks, which never came.*

An extract of Prince Albert's account provides a glimpse of the action:

I was in A Turret and watched most of the action through one of the trainer's telescopes as we were firing by Director, when the turret trained in the working chamber and not in the gun house. At the commencement I was sitting on the top of A Turret and had a very good view of proceedings. I was up there during a lull, when a German ship started firing at us, and one salvo straddled us. We at once returned the fire. I was distinctly startled and jumped down the hole in the top of the turret like a shot rabbit! I didn't try the experience again. The ship was in a fine state on the main deck. Inches of water sluicing about to prevent fires from getting a hold on deck. Most of the cabins were also flooded.

The hands behaved splendidly and all of them in the best of spirits as their heart's desire had at last been granted, which was to be in action with the Germans. Some of the turret's crew actually took bets with one another that we should not fire a shot. A good deal of money must have changed hands I should think by now.

My impressions were very different to what I expected. I saw visions of the masts going over the side and funnels hurtling through the air etc. In reality none of these things happened and we are still quite sound as before. No one would know to look at the ship that we had been in action. It was certainly a great experience to have been through and it shows that we are at war and that the Germans can fight if they like.

After waiting in vain for the Germans to reappear and continue the battle off Jutland, the Grand Fleet returned to Scapa. Three days later Lord Kitchener embarked upon his fateful mission to Russia. As the cruiser *Hampshire* passed through the ships of the Fleet, *Collingwood* amongst them, the men cheered and cheered again as the tall grey figure on the bridge in field uniform, his greatcoat buttoned around him, stood at the salute. A heavy sea was running, so heavy that the *Hampshire's* destroyer escort was compelled to turn back almost immediately. A few hours later, within sight of the Orkneys, the cruiser struck a mine, and in fifteen minutes had disappeared, taking her ship's company of 800 officers and men, and the Field Marshal and his staff. This tragedy will have weighed heavily after the excitement of battle. To the great majority of Englishmen, the term K still retained that magic quality which had raised the First Hundred Thousand.

Eric, Henry's older brother had been one of those who had answered Kitchener's first call to arms. Four months after the loss of the *Hampshire*, on the 15 October 1916, Eric died from a headwound sustained at the Battle of Fleurs-Courcelette, part of the Somme offensive. Henry and the rest of the family were bereft.

In December 1916 Prince Albert wrote to Henry in the *Collingwood* from Admiralty House, Portsmouth to report his progress in trying to hasten Henry's next appointment. Perhaps the warmth of his greeting *My Dear Old Jimmy* stemmed from his concern for his friend's recent loss and the camaraderie engendered from serving together in Turret A at the Battle of Jutland.

Admiralty House
Portsmouth
20th December 1916
My Dear Old Jimmy

> *Very many thanks for your letter. I went straight to the Admiral and put everything about you before him. He telephoned up to Buller[14] at the Admiralty at once, and Buller said he'd appoint you to one as soon as possible. So I think by the time you receive this, you ought to have received your appointment.*
>
> *I mentioned a Harwich destroyer as I thought that was the place where most things were likely to happen from[14]. So if all this comes off all right, I wish you the best of luck in the future. It has taken a long time to work, hasn't it? But still it ought to be all right now. I know I was very thankful when I left the ship. 3 years is too long to be in one ship. One only gets bored to death with one's surroundings.*
>
> *Down here I am very well billeted and until I get to sea again, it will keep me employed. I see several friends here and a few of our term who are doing submarines. I saw Cavendish 10 days ago, but haven't heard what he is going to do now.*
>
> *Murray the flag Lieut here was in the same term as Harries[14]. He is a ripping fellow and I have made great friends with him. I saw AK Gibson[14] a short time ago. Very flourishing as usual. He has got a TB at Newhaven. He comes for a refit here next month, so I hope to see him again then.*
>
> *I heard all about Jimmy Ley's departure to 'the Canada'. I am so glad to hear you like Nicholson[14]. What a change it must be not having a flap every 5 minutes! Many thanks for your good wishes for my birthday. Will you please thank the Gunroom for the Xmas card and give them all my best wishes for Xmas and New Year. Well hoping this letter will buck you up and my very best wishes for Xmas and the New Year.*
>
> *I remain*
> *Ever*
> *Yours very sincerely*
> *Albert*
> *PS Do write and let me know what destroyer you get!*

1917–1919. HMS *Redoubt*
Destroyer R Class. Aged 21–23

(displacement tonnage 1,073; overall length x breadth 274 x 27 ft; Doxford 28.10.1916)
Clearly Prince Albert's efforts on Henry's behalf had the desired effect and after what must have been a sad family Christmas at Aylestone Hill, Hereford, Henry joined HMS *Redoubt* as First Lieutenant on 1 February 1917 at Harwich.

According to *Royal Naval Records* and *Ships Histories* there were only two episodes about the *Redoubt* during the next two and a half years which seem to have been worth recording. The first occurred within three months of Henry joining the ship when on the 18 April 1917, the *Redoubt* collided with the Coal Hulk *Himalaya* when leaving Harwich Harbour at night and subsequently underwent repairs at Chatham. The findings of the Court of Enquiry held between the 19 and 25 April, show no sign of Henry being called as a witness, which implies he was not on duty at the time. Lieutenant Commander RV Holt seems to have taken some responsibility for the collision, which was caused by a Signalman not reading a signal correctly.

Unlike the first rather chastening experience, the second from *Ships Histories* records an early courageous experiment in aircraft carrier tactics.

On the evening of 10th August 1918, the Harwich Force put to sea. *Redoubt* was towing a lighter with the aeroplane, three other destroyers had flying boats on lighters astern. The next morning the Zeppelin L53 was sighted flying at a great height. *Redoubt* turned into the wind and Lieutenant S D Culley took off in pursuit, reaching 19,000 ft an hour later; he opened fire and in a few minutes the airship was a mass of flames. Culley ditched near *Redoubt*, and the fighter was fished out of the water and placed on the lighter for return to base.

Lighters had a 30ft deck in order to fly off a Sopwith Camel fighter.

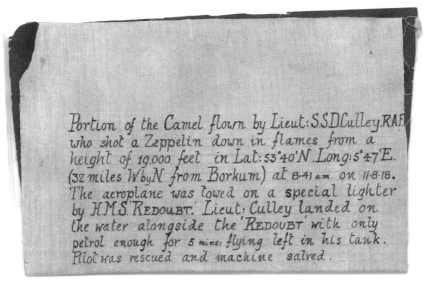

Portion of the Camel flown by Lieut: S.S.D.Culley.RAF who shot a Zeppelin down in flames from a height of 19,000 feet in Lat: 53°40'N Long: 5°47'E. (32 miles WbyN from Borkum) at 8·41 a.m. on 11·8·18. The aeroplane was towed on a special lighter by HMS 'REDOUBT'. Lieut: Culley landed on the water alongside the 'REDOUBT' with only petrol enough for 5 mins: flying left in his tank. Pilot was rescued and machine salved.

31. Fabric from Lieutenant Culley's Sopwith Camel; HMS *Redoubt* 1918.

Henry, who must have been keen to keep a memento of this action, sent a piece of fabric from the Camel's fuselage home to his parents.[15]

By then everyone was longing for peace and finally on 11 November 1918 Armistice was declared – the end of the First World War.

Between the Wars

Henry continued serving in the *Redoubt* for a further year, this time in a peace time Royal Navy, cruising as undisputed rulers of the high seas. In July 1919 he heard again from Prince Albert replying to his letter from Sydney, Cape Breton Island.

Buckingham Palace
London
12th July 1919
Dear James

> *Very many thanks for your letter from Sydney, Cape Breton Island* [16]. *It is ages since we have seen each other, something like two and a half years. I think the last time was at Portsmouth in the Dockyard one forenoon for about two minutes.*
> *I am very flourishing but very busy in London doing all kinds of things. My flying days are nearly over now. I am giving up a service career and am taking up my public duties. There is so much going on and my brother can't do it all, so I am going to help him with it. Personally I am very pleased as I could never have gone on in the RAF and I should have been too terribly rusty to have gone back to sea. But I am never leaving the Navy properly. In fact I shall be in both the Navy and the Air Force without actually doing anything in either.*
> *I am going to Cambridge in October to learn all about political economy etc. This will take a year to do properly and then I suppose I shall always be doing something or going somewhere all my life.*
> *I wonder whether you will go on in the Service. I suppose so anyhow for a time, as the Navy is always bound to be what she was before the War. How long is your cruise for and when do you think of getting home again? Do let me know as we might be able to arrange a meeting some time.*
> *This is all my own news and what is happening to me.*
> *The best of luck to you.*
> *Ever*
> *Yours very sincerely*
> *Albert*

A month later on 19 August 1919, Henry joined HMS *Temeraire* as a Lieutenant.

1919–1921. HMS Temeraire
Battleship. Aged 23–24

(displacement tonnage 18,600; overall length x breadth 490 x 82.5 ft; armament ten 12 in; sixteen 4 in; Devonport Dockyard 24.8.1907)

In the Spring of 1920 the media became aware that Prince George, together with 120 of his term at Dartmouth, would be going on a seven month cruise in the *Temeraire* between June and December 1920. In May Prince Albert wrote to Henry asking him if he would keep an eye on his younger brother, later to become the Duke of Kent.

Southacre
Cambridge
12th May 1920
My dear James

> *As you know my brother George is joining the Temeraire for the next cruise, so I am writing to ask you if you will send for him occasionally and find out how he is getting on. He may be in your division no doubt, and I expect you will teach him seamanship etc. He has kept up the best traditions of my family by passing out from Dartmouth one from bottom, the same place as I did!*
> *I hope you had a good cruise in the West Indies, revisiting our haunts of a few years ago. I heard from Spencer-Cooper at Bermuda that he had seen you there. What day do you go off again this time? About 1st June, isn't it?*

32. HMS *Temeraire*.

Do let me know how you are.
Ever
Yours
Albert

Naval Cadet Training Cruise, June–December 1920

Itinerary: Portsmouth–Dunmore (Ireland)–Galway–Killery
Bay–Buncrana–Campbeltown–Lochbroom–Stornaway–Scapa–Odda–Bergen–
Trondjeim–Rosyth–Vigo–Gibraltar–Algiers–Malta–Palma–Gibraltar–Lisbon–Arosa
Bay–Torquay–Portsmouth.

The Report on the Cruise provides a detailed account of the next seven months, most of which is of little interest. However it is clear from correspondence beforehand, that no less than three itineraries were proposed before agreement was reached. Moreover the tone of Captain Donaldson's letters beforehand seemed to put people on edge. His determination that Prince George was to be treated as a normal cadet did not sit comfortably with his request that special expenses for entertainment should be allowed. After this was ultimately but reluctantly agreed, preparations became more harmonious.

A selection of entries in Cruise Report give some flavour of events:

17 June 1920. Buncrana. Condition of Londonderry was very bad during our stay at Buncrana. Constant fighting taking place. No leave to Londonderry was given.

21 August 1920. King Haakon of Norway inspects HMS *Temeraire*. Twenty one gun salute. He graciously informed me (Captain L Donaldson CMG) that he thought the officers and men were smart and that the ship was very clean. Prince George stays with their Majesties at Konsgaard (Summer Residence) returning on board every morning at 9 o'clock.

2 September 1920. Christiania. Extract from letter from British Legation to Right Honourable The Earl Curzon of Kedleston KG.

Their Majesties entertained the Captain and principal officers at a Dinner at Kongsgaard and again on the eve of departure of the vessel. They also gave an afternoon dance for the Cadets.

Their Majesties were also pleased to honour Lady Findlay and myself by bringing Prince George to tea in the garden of the Legation and watched various games of tennis between the officers and cadets with interest.

Lady Findlay gave a small dance at the Legation for the cadets and we had also the pleasure of seeing Captain Donaldson and some of his officers at Dinner on two occasions while the officers and cadets almost daily turned up to tea and tennis. His Majesty's Consul, Mr E F Gray also entertained the officers and cadets on several occasions and Mrs Gray was most helpful in finding Norwegian girls to be invited to dance on board.

The proprietor of the Chat Noire Music Hall invited 150 officers, petty officers and men to his performance which was much appreciated, a bottle of champagne being provided gratis between two guests.

His Majesty King Haakon inspected the ship as a British Admiral and Their Majesties were also present at a most successful dance given on board after the conclusion of the Cadets' Examinations.

I understand that the Norwegian girls who were invited were not acquainted with the 'Malita' and other complicated dances popular on the lower deck.

Just before the departure of the Temeraire, Their Majesties went on board to take leave of Prince George and of the ship.

M de C Findlay

British Legation

Lecture by Captain E R G (Teddy) Evans, who had been Captain Scott's second-in-command during the ill-fated Terra Nova Antarctic Expedition of 1910-1913.

Visits to Algiers and Lisbon were cancelled due to outbreaks of Bubonic Plague within the Ports.

During the latter part of the cruise Henry received two further letters from Prince Albert:

Buckingham Palace

London

11th November 1920

My dear James

Ever so very many thanks for your letter and the photograph (perhaps of Prince George?).

I am so glad to hear my brother is getting on well. I heard from him the other day and he seemed to be having a pretty good time and enjoying himself. It must be very interesting work seeing how the cadets grow up, when you can well remember being one yourself. Do you have much to do with them, or are you a watchkeeper?

When you come home in December, if you are going to be in London at all, do let me know and let us arrange to have a meeting somewhere. It is ages since we met, the last time I think was at Portsmouth in 1917. So much has happened to both of us in the last 3 years, & it will be nice to have a talk about old times. You were lucky meeting so many old friends from the 'Collingwood' at Malta. Tait, as you know got married, & has now got a daughter which arrived the other day. Rolleston[17] left the Service & his family has remained in Australia. He was in the ' Renown'& was no great loss to them. I never

Many thanks for your card

WITH BEST WISHES

FOR

A MERRY XMAS

AND

A HAPPY NEW YEAR

1920 - 21

Albert

33. Christmas Card 1920–21 to Henry from Prince Albert.
34. Opposite: Henry, Mary and John at Tidnacott, 1921.

thought very much of him, did you? Cavendish, I understand, has also left and Herbert[17] is going to be married & leaves the Service on the strength of it.
I am kept pretty busy here now in one way or another, so do not get much time to myself.
The best of luck to you & hoping we shall meet on your return.
Ever
Yours very sincerely
Albert

Buckingham Palace
8th December 1920
My Dear James
Now that you are home once more, do let me know when you are coming up to London so that we can arrange a meeting[18].
I shall be here till about the 22nd, but may be away from the 17th till the 20th of this month. My brother seems very well, but looking rather thin.
So long
Ever
Yours truly,
Albert

After this Christmas card, Henry's papers do not contain any further letters from Prince Albert until 1938. Quite possibly there were none. Alternatively, and as is more likely, those letters written during the next 18 years were lost, together with Henry's other belongings, when Gieves depository in London, where his belongings were stored, was destroyed by fire during the blitz.

During the period 1921 to 1925 Henry served as a Lieutenant for seven months in the depot ship HMS *Colleen* in Queenstown and then for two years throughout 1922 and 1923 in HMS *Vancouver*, a VW Class Destroyer. Between January 1924 and April 1925 he served in HMS *Versatile*, also a VW Class Destroyer. During 1924 the *Versatile* completed a Spring cruise to Spanish ports, followed by a refit at Chatham and cruising in home coastal waters. In early 1925 she once again cruised to Spanish ports and while at Gibraltar, Henry wrote home to his mother and father.

HMS Versatile
1st Destroyer Flotilla
c/o GPO
At Gibraltar
27th February 1925
My darling Mother & Father,

Very many thanks indeed for your letter. Am so glad you are enjoying your visits. Great news today. I was in the 'Wallace' this morning & Captain (D) told me I have got my first Destroyer in command. I do not yet know the name of it, but it will be one of those in reserve at Port Edgar – a destroyer in reserve is always one's first command. It is rather funny, but all the first lieutenants in the First Flotilla seem to be getting their commands before anyone else.

Succeeded in doing a perfect Night Full calibre Divisional Concentration two nights ago–hit the target the first salvo & kept on hitting. We have got Captain D's firing coming off some time next week. There is great keenness over this, as there is a trophy (a silver model of a 4 in gun) for the best destroyer. 'Versatile' hope to walk off with this as well.

Must say bye bye darling, as am very busy.

Very best love
Ever yr very aff: son,
Henry

After a further four months in HMS *Shakespeare*, a destroyer of the 9th Flotilla Atlantic Fleet, on 14 August 1925 Henry took over command of HMS *Stormcloud*, an S Class Destroyer and three months later was promoted Lieutenant Commander.

1925–1929. HMS *Stormcloud*
S Class Destroyer, in Command. Aged 29–33
(displacement tonnage 1,075; overall length x breadth 273 x 27.25 ft; armament three 4 in; one 2 pdr pom pom; Palmer 30.5.1919)

For the next four years Henry will have been in his element, while commanding his first destroyer, while serving in Home Waters and the China Seas, as part of the 8th Flotilla Atlantic Fleet. In the absence of evidence to the contrary, we must assume that although an unforgettable experience for Henry, this will have been mainly routine seagoing naval service, but none the worse for that.

However in April and October 1927 there were two incidents involving *Stormcloud* near Hong Kong, which Henry and his ship's company must have found exciting and received some coverage in the newspapers in England. Piracy in the China Seas was common at the time.

35. HMS *Stormcloud* 1925.

36. Henry with his ships company, HMS *Stormcloud*, China Seas 1927.

Extract from the Yorkshire Post 18 April 1927

Warships Fine Rescue

British Bluejackets carry Women and Children to Safety

In spite of the rough weather, which made rescue more difficult, HM destroyer *Stormcloud* has now succeeded in taking off all the passengers from the Dutch passenger vessel, *Tjilboet* which went ashore near here yesterday. The rescued passengers are being brought to Hong Kong.

The rescue of the passengers was particularly onerous, owing to the fact that the Chinese appeared to be absolutely incapable of helping themselves. Bluejackets carried the women and children from the *Tjilboet* to the boats and again from the boats to the tugs and on board the *Stormcloud*. The *Tjikarang*, a sister ship of the damaged steamer, is standing by ready to send out the SOS if pirates appear on the scene. One of HM destroyers is also ready to give assistance if necessary. *Reuter.*

Extract from the *Daily Mail* 22 October 1927

From Our Own Correspondent

Hong Kong, Friday

A sensational naval capture of a number of pirates from the notorious Bias Bay district near Hong Kong was made on Thursday night.

The Chinese steamer *Irene*, which had left Hong Kong for Amoy on Wednesday, was several hours from the former port when Chinese pirates, who boarded her disguised as passengers, seized the ship.

The outlaws forced six European and many Chinese below. They then cruised about during the day not wishing to approach Bias Bay before nightfall. Suddenly the *Irene* was accosted by a British submarine, the L4. The ship failed to answer the challenge of the submarine. The latter then fired shots into her hull, disabling the engine, and setting fire to the vessel.

The officers, crew and passengers were rescued from the ship with the assistance of HMS *Delhi*, cruiser; HMS *Stormcloud*, destroyer, and HMS *Magnolia*, sloop, and were brought to Hong Kong.

Out of a crew of approximately 260, 24 passengers remained unaccounted for. Most of the pirates were captured. The *Irene*, waterlogged, has been taken into Bias Bay.

Great heroism was displayed by sailors in the British warships. They repeatedly dived overboard to save passengers struggling in the water.

According to Navy Lists, Henry handed over command of HMS *Stormcloud* after three and a half years at the end of March 1929. He then took some

37. Henry with his mother and her father, Bill Waddon-Martyn .
38. Henry holds June atop a stone pillar at Tidnacott, 1929.

well earned home leave with the family during that summer. The next two photographs, above, capture the scene in Cornwall.

1929–1932. HMS Antelope
Acasta Class Destroyer. Aged 34–36
(displacement tonnage 1,350; overall length x breadth 323 x 32.5 ft; armament four 4.7 in QF; two 2 pdr pom pom; four Lewis guns; eight tt; Hawthorn Leslie Newcastle-on-Tyne 27.7.1929)

On 2 December 1929 Henry took over command of HMS *Antelope*, which had only been launched the previous July. Henry must have been delighted at becoming her first commander. He will have noticed several design and operational improvements by comparison with HMS *Stormcloud*, which by then had been in service for ten years.

During the next two years the *Antelope*, Henry's second command, served mostly in the Mediterranean.

1932–1933. HMS Pembroke
Nominal base ship at Royal Naval Barracks, Chatham. Aged 36–37

Towards the end of 1931 Henry received the excellent news that on 31 December he would be promoted to Commander and that in May 1932 he would take over command of the Royal Naval Barracks, Chatham, often referred to in naval circles as HMS *Pembroke*. An extract from *The Times* of 31 December 1931 made it official:

NEW DRAFTING COMMANDER RN BARRACKS, CHATHAM AFTER COMMANDING DESTROYER ANTELOPE IN THE MEDITERRANEAN

Commander James entered Osborne as a cadet in January 1909 in the same term as the Duke of York and served during the war as Midshipman and Sub Lieutenant of the Battleship *Collingwood*, to which the Duke was also appointed. After the Battle of Jutland, Commander James became First Lieutenant of the Destroyer *Redoubt* in which he served for two years. From 1925 to 1929 he commanded the Destroyer *Stormcloud* in Home Waters and in the China Seas.

In January 1932 Henry handed over command of the *Antelope,* and after some home leave he took over command of RN Barracks Chatham on 7 May 1932.

39. Opposite: HMS *Antelope* at
a port in the Mediterranean.

40. Henry leaves Aylestone Hill
to command RN Barracks,
Chatham May 1932.

Henry's next eighteen months at Chatham required leadership, hard
work and attention to detail, but in the main followed an established
routine. His Record of Service does not indicate that anything of major
significance occurred during his tour. In October 1933 he handed over to his
successor and took up his next appointment as Director of Personal Services
at the Ministry of Defence on 24 November 1933 at the age of thirty seven.
His sea going experience had now been supplemented by two key shore
appointments which showed him to be an able Staff Officer. By the time he
handed over to his successor just over two years later in January 1936, he
must have been encouraged by how his career was progressing. After nearly
four years ashore he looked forward to returning to sea.

1936–1938. HMS Fearless
Destroyer. Aged 39–41
(displacement tonnage 1,375; overall length x breadth 329 x 33.25 ft; armament four
4.7 in; eight tt; Cammell Laird 12.5.1934)
On 3 January 1936 Henry took over command of HMS *Fearless*, the leader of
a Division of the 6th Destroyer Flotilla Home Fleet. This Fleet consisted of

40 Destroyers deployed on anti-piracy patrol off the Spanish coast. Their main task was the evacuation of refugees and the general protection of British interests during the Spanish Civil War. Undoubtedly much of this patrolling was monotonous, but in 1937 HMS *Fearless* was involved in two incidents which attracted public attention and were reported in the press.

In August 1937 HMS *Fearless* and HMS *Foxhound*, who were based in Devonport, were tasked to undertake non-intervention patrolling along the northern coast of Spain. This involved spending about seven days at sea and five in port, ensuring that merchant ships entering Spanish waters were carrying non-intervention officers and checking that their cargoes to ensure that they did not contain war material for Spain.

Off the port of Gijon there were invariably two insurgent trawlers and a cruiser. Outside the three mile limit of Spanish territorial waters were usually a group of merchant ships, including the British, which were awaiting the opportunity to dodge the insurgent vessels and enter Gijon, in the possession of Government forces. It was in this grim game of 'running the gauntlet' that *Fearless* took part. It was her duty to intervene when, occasionally, insurgent warships menaced vessels outside the three mile limit.

The first incident was when the two Spanish insurgent trawlers fired warning shots and ordered the British Steamer *Bramhill* to stop, considering her to be within the three mile limit. *Bramhill's* officers did not agree they were so did not stop, but called for assistance. HMS *Fearless* arrived to investigate, and on two occasions Henry gave the order to clear for action. On both occasions potential engagements were avoided after an exchange of signals. In the words of the report transmitted to the Admiralty, 'after an exchange of signals the incident was closed.'

41. HMS *Fearless*.

The second incident was when HMS *Fearless* was bombed, which was reported in extracts from *The Observer* and *The Western Morning News*:

from *The Observer* 19 September 1937

BOMBS NEAR BRITISH DESTROYER

ATTACK OFF SPAIN COAST

It was confirmed at the Admiralty yesterday that HM Destroyer *Fearless* (1,375 tons), on patrol on the north coast of Spain, has reported being attacked on Friday at about midday, by an aeroplane, which dropped six heavy bombs close by.

The ship was not hit, and there were no casualties.

The aeroplane was not identified, but it returned in the direction of Gijon, which is in Red hands.

Fearless's foregun is painted red, white and blue so that she can be identified as a British ship.

The Western Morning News 26 October 1937

'FEARLESS' BOMBED

The bombing of *Fearless* was the work of the Spanish Government plane from Gijon, which, apparently, mistook the destroyer for a Spanish insurgent vessel.

A total of six missiles were dropped. The nearest was within 50 yards of the ship and the farthest 150 yards distant. Subsequently, splinters were found in many parts of the ship, including the bridge.

A stoker petty officer, standing near one of the vessel's quadruple mounts of torpedo tubes, discovered that his overcoat had been rent by one splinter, which he found in his pocket.

There were, however, no personal injuries. The general opinion of the crew was that the bombing, undertaken from a great height was very accurate.

To avoid repetition of the attack, the Captain went full steam ahead.

Such incidents would have relieved months of monotony. The sailors, never lacking in initiative, had purchased 'spinners' from French ports. By simply dropping these over the side of the ship, they could haul aboard tunny averaging 7 lbs in weight. A welcome supplement to ships rations.

During November 1937, some months after The Duke of York had been crowned King, Henry wrote to a friend in Buckingham Palace to discover the name of the King's Private Secretary and how Henry should now address the King when writing to him. This was his reply:

44 Eaton Place
London SW1
2nd December 1937
Dear James
    I have returned home to find your letter & please excuse haste & brevity in
    reply as am about to leave London again.
    H H Hardinge is The King's Private Secretary.
    Letters should be addressed:
                The King
                Buckingham Palace
                London SW1
    I should start:
                Sir
                May I write to thank ...
and end:
                I have the honour to be, Sir,
                Your Loyal & Obedient Servant
    My very best wishes to you
    Yours sincerely
    HG Campbell

Henry handed over command of HMS *Fearless* in December 1937, having
heard that his next appointment would be with Operations Division, Naval
Staff at the Ministry of Defence, starting on 18 January 1938. There was a
brief entry in The Times:

The Times, 19 January 1938
    Commander PHG James has joined the Staff of the Operations
    Division, Admiralty on relinquishing command of *Fearless*. He has had
    former Admiralty service in Personal Services.

Six months later on 30 June 1938, Henry was promoted to Captain and
appointed President (Operations Division) at the age of forty two. On the
following day he received a telegram from His Majesty, The King.

    His tour with Operations Division finished three months later and on
28 September he took over command of HMS *Mackay* (Leader Class
destroyer) for an interim eleven days.

Opposite:
42. Henry's telegram of congratulations from His Majesty, King George VI.
43. Henry at the German Club, Shanghai on German National Day, 1939.

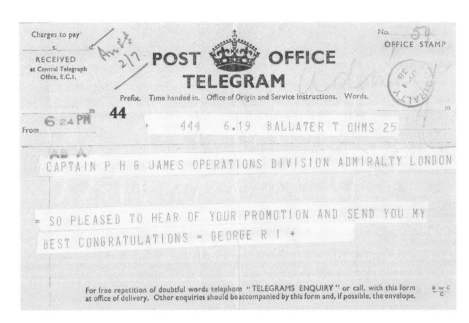

January 1939–October 1940 Naval Liaison Officer, Shanghai
Aged 42–44

After some home leave, on 1 December 1938 Henry was appointed to HMS *Cumberland* as Naval Liaison Officer, Shanghai. He took up this extremely sensitive post on 1 January 1939, just as another war with Germany was becoming increasingly likely.

During his next twenty two months as Naval Liaison Officer in Shanghai, Henry needed to exercise his relaxed charm, tact and diplomatic restraint in his dealings with the Japanese authorities, who at the time were becoming increasingly assertive and intractable.

Second World War

3 September 1939 Outbreak of the Second World War

After a year in post Henry received a most encouraging letter from Admiral Sir Percy Noble, which he promptly sent home to his parents, saying *I have never received such a charming letter of appreciation before – it helps one in one's future endeavours.*

31st December 1939
My Dear James

> *I write on the last day of the year to assure you of the fact that I have very greatly appreciated the excellent work that you have done and are doing since you took over your most difficult appointment. The tenacity of purpose with which you have kept up a continuous attack – the tact with which you have handled the many intricate problems that we have given you, will not be forgotten and will be reported in the proper quarter.*
> *In particular your work with Admiral (Censored)… has been most successful and must I am sure, be a source of gratification to yourself. While I write I have a paper before me in which … (Censored)… and this in my opinion, is entirely due to your efforts and influence.*
> *I hope that when you are able to go to Tokyo, you will find it not only of interest from the service point of view, but also a slight holiday which I know you fully deserve.*
> *All my good wishes for 1940 and again my sincere thanks*
> *Yours very sincerely*
> *Admiral Sir Percy Noble*

The outbreak of war in the Mediterranean on 10 June 1940, when Italy under Mussolini, joined Hitler's axis troops against the British and Commonwealth forces, prompted the need to increase Royal Naval resources in both the Mediterranean and the East Indies. Despite the priority call to defend supply convoys in the North Atlantic, there was a steady reinforcement of these increasingly important theatres of operations during the next six months. By June 1940 Henry had been in Shanghai eighteen months so he, and so many other Royal Naval Captains from around the world, were soon to learn that their next posting would be to command their next ship in this region.

By Autumn 1940 Henry may well have felt that it was high time to move on from Naval Liaison duties in Shanghai to see a bit of action. Learning that he would take over command of the Light Cruiser HMS *Capetown* in the East Indies in early November would have been an exciting prospect. Nevertheless it was essential that he devoted all his energies to his liaison duties until then. An extract from Henry's Confidential Report written three days after he handed over to his successor on 25 October 1940, shows how the British Embassy valued his performance:

To be noted in the record of Captain P H G James RN

British Embassy
Shanghai
28th October 1940

> *I have the honour to report that Captain P H G James relinquished his appointment as Naval Liaison Officer attached to this Embassy on the 25th October on transfer to other duties.*
>
> *Captain James took over the post of Naval Liaison Officer on 1st January 1939. In the subsequent twenty two months he has often been called upon to handle difficult and delicate questions, many of them involving intricate negotiations with the local Japanese authorities, who are not at the best of times very easy to deal with. In these difficult circumstances it says much for Captain James' pertinacity and tact that he has been able to achieve as much as he has in protecting British interests from high handed action by the Japanese naval authorities and in smoothing over the difficulties which were inevitable in dealing with such childishly sensitive people as the Japanese. Captain James has been able at the same time to maintain the most friendly personal relations with the Japanese officials with whom he has had to deal.*
>
> *Captain James has had much work to do and has cheerfully worked at all hours of the day and night to get through it. I greatly regret the departure of so able an officer, whose services have been of great value not only to this Embassy but also to His Majesty's Consul General here.*
>
> *Captain James has been most efficiently supported by Lieutenant Commander Sheppard RN who is now taking over the duties of Naval Liaison Officer and whose knowledge of the Japanese language and psychology has been and will be*

44. Henry hands over to Lieutenant Commander Sheppard, October 1940.

45. HMS *Capetown* at Nancowry in the Nicobar Islands.

of great assistance to this Embassy.
This dispatch is necessarily written in the absence of His Majesty's
Ambassador, but I am sure that His Excellency would fully endorse all that I
have said.
I have the honour to be etc
Signed P M Broadhead

November 1940–June 1941. HMS *Capetown*
Light Cruiser, in Command. Aged 44–45

(Carlisle cls cruiser; displacement tonnage 4,190; overall length x breadth 451.5 x
43.9 ft; top speed 29 knots; complement 437; armament five 6 in, two 3 in, eight 21
in tt; Cammell Laird Birkenhead 28.6.1919)

Henry had just ten days leave between handing over his liaison duties in
Shanghai on 25 October and taking over command of HMS *Capetown* in
Colombo on 4 November. Bearing in mind communications at the time,
this would have meant a brief spell of local leave before reporting
for duty.

Henry had an inauspicious start to his service in HMS *Capetown* for
within twelve days of taking over command of this twenty year old Light
Cruiser, she ran aground at Nancowry in the Nicobar Islands in the Indian
Ocean on 16 November. Admiralty Letter N.L. 3362/41 of 7 April 1941,
which is attached to Henry's confidential report, sheds some light on
what happened:

> **In connection with the grounding of HMS *Capetown* at Nancowry on 16**
> **November 1940.** Captain James was held to blame for the following reasons:
> (a) the selection of Beresford Channel as an anchorage rather than Cross
> Harbour was unwise.
> (b) immediately on anchoring, the engines were rung off and no respon-
> sible officer remained on the bridge, or leadsman in the chains, to ensure
> that the ship swung to her cable and brought up.
> (c) although certain shoals were visible (the sun being astern) no steps
> were taken to send a special lookout aloft to assist in keeping the ship in
> deep water.
> The Commander-in-Chief, East Indies was accordingly requested to con-
> vey to Captain P H G James RN an award of Their Lordships' displeasure.

According to *Ships Histories*, HMS *Capetown* was on ocean convoy escort
and raider hunting duties based mainly in Colombo until early 1941, when
she took part in the blockade of Italian Somaliland between 9 and 16
February. After boiler cleaning in Mombasa, she joined the search for the
pocket battleship Admiral Scheer in March, and was sent to the Red Sea as

part of the force blockading the Eritrean Coast, and also escorting convoys passing through the area.

A brief extract from *The Chronology of the War at Sea 1939–1945* provides a useful insight into the Royal Navy's supporting role against Italian Somaliland:

> **10–25 February 1941.** To support British offensive against Somaliland from Kenya, Vice Admiral Leatham formed Force T with cruiser *Shropshire*, the carrier *Hermes*, the old cruisers *Hawkins*, *Capetown* and *Ceres* and the destroyer *Kandahar*. They supported the advance on land with their fire.

A second extract from the same source also describes the final battle for the Italian base of Massawa[19] in Eritrea, in which HMS *Capetown*, under Henry's command, took a leading role:

> **1–8 April 1941 East Africa/Red Sea. Final battle for the base of Massawa (Eritrea).** After the destroyer *Leone*, which went aground on 31 March, is destroyed by her own crew, the remaining seaworthy destroyers *Pantera*, *Manin*, *Sauro* and *Battisti* put to sea on 2 April to attack Port Sudan. Captain Gasparini is in command of the operation. *Battisti* has soon to remain behind because of engine trouble and scuttles herself the next day off the Arabian Coast. On the same day aircraft from the British carrier *Eagle*, taking off from shore bases, attack the remaining force about 10 nautical miles off Port Sudan and sink *Manin* and *Sauro*. The other two destroyers are able to get away and then scuttle themselves off the Arabian Coast. After the defenders of Massawa have beaten off some attacks the enemy begins his attack on 6 April, following sea and air bombardment. This leads two days later to the fall of the town.

An extract from *Ships Histories* records how on 8 April, the last day of the battle, HMS *Capetown* is torpedoed off the harbour of Mersa Kuba:

> On 8 April 1941, while escorting a convoy, *Capetown* was attacked and torpedoed by an Italian motor torpedo boat. The torpedo struck on the starboard side abreast B boiler room, which immediately flooded. All power and lighting failed, but the flooding was checked and the cruiser was taken in tow by the Australian sloop *Parramatta*. *Capetown*, still in tow, arrived at Port Sudan, 294 miles north of the scene of the attack on 10 April.
>
> After some doubt as to whether she was repairable, emergency repairs were made to make her fit for a passage under tow to Bombay. This passage took place between 5 and 20 May, the tug *Tai Koo* towing *Capetown*.

The damage to HMS *Capetown* was substantial and consisted of a hole 16 feet long by 13 feet deep. Inevitably such a large explosion in a boiler room caused casualties. The five ratings occupying it were killed outright; one Goanese Petty Officer was lost overboard and one Marine subsequently died of internal injuries. There were six other minor casualties.

Fortunately the crew's damage control response at 2.15 am on the 8 April was exemplary. This not only saved the ship, but after emergency repairs in Port Sudan, she was then towed 720 miles to Aden and finally a further 1657 miles via Masirah and Karachi to Bombay for repair. Being under tow for a total of 2671 miles was a remarkable feat of seamanship.

A Court of Enquiry was convened on 3 June to enquire into the torpedoing of HMS *Capetown* on 7/8 April 1941. As ship's Captain, Henry was naturally required to produce his report of this incident and some extracts from a copy of his 13 page report dated 5 May 1941, are shown at Appendix 3 at the end of this section. While much of it is technical, it provides a good insight into the circumstances beforehand and the response to the attack. It is an impressive document and makes interesting reading. Some extracts from the Findings of the Court of Enquiry are shown below:

Extract from Report of Findings of the Court of Enquiry held on board HMS Emerald on 3rd June 1941 to enquire into the torpedoing of HMS Capetown off Massawa on 7/8th April 1941

3. The distance from Massawa was only 40 miles, and the enemy was presumably aware of the operation, and the moon silhouetted HMS *Capetown* to vessels seaward. Conditions were therefore ideal for attack. Captain James has explained that in deciding to keep *Parramatta* and *Indus* at anchor he was influenced by the necessity for conserving fuel. For the same reason, and to avoid creating a wash at the unloading pier, HMS *Capetown* herself patrolled at a speed of only eight knots. His desire to keep close support to the convoy, coupled with the limited area swept for mines, caused Captain James to maintain a regular patrol. The Auxiliaries *El Kebir* and *El Affia* were not used for warning patrols as they were watering and also assisting with unloading – a matter of great urgency. Without outside evidence as to the urgency of this operation balanced against the likelihood of attack, we do not consider ourselves in a position to criticise Captain James on the above matter. The only criticism we wish to make as to the steps taken to avoid surprise attack is that we think more definite instructions might usefully have been given to *Parramatta* and *Indus* to maintain a constant Asdic listening watch for surface vessels.

4. We are of the opinion that HMS *Capetown* was in a proper state of alertness and that the torpedo could not have been avoided when sighted. We consider that the action taken subsequent to the explosion

46. Henry on the Quarter Deck of
HMS *Capetown* in the Indian Ocean.

47. Hole in HMS *Capetown* viewed from
dockside looking forward.

was correct and efficient and indicates that the damage control training
in HMS *Capetown* had reached a high standard.

Forwarding Findings and Minutes of Board of Enquiry: Extract
2. The very urgent needs of the army in Eritrea are confirmed and
justified the unloading operation at Kuba continuing throughout the
night. The three remaining Italian destroyers *Battisti, Orsini* and *Acerbi*
had not definitely been located and it was reasonable to assume they
might be at Massawa or among the islands. Only *Capetown* could provide
adequate protection for the ships and base against a destroyer attack and
it was therefore right that *Capetown* should have remained on patrol in
the vicinity. Although no offensive activity of E boats had even been
apparent it was considered that there were still four or five at Massawa.
I consider therefore that Captain James should have stationed both sloops
as a screen to seaward of himself for the greater security of *Capetown*
against these boats and suchlike.
The desire to conserve the fuel of the sloops so that the army could later
on be helped to the utmost is understandable but in the circumstances it
should not have been allowed to override the need for taking all possible

precautions. I consider Captain James' judgement was at fault in this respect and have informed him accordingly, but it cannot be said that, had he decided differently, the torpedo would not still have reached its mark.

3. The reports show that the ship was in an alert state at the time of the attack and that the internal organisation was satisfactory. The initiative displayed in the engine room department was praiseworthy.

Commander-in-Chief, East Indies Station
19 June 1941

As a consequence of this finding, a note was placed on Henry's Confidential Report in similar vein:

In connection with the torpedoing of HMS Capetown on 8th April 1941. Their Lordships stated that since there was reason to believe that there were E boats and other vessels at Massawa and HMS *Capetown* silhouetted to seaward by the moon, they consider that at least one of the sloops available should have been stationed as an off shore screen and that his desire to conserve fuel of the sloops should not have been allowed to override this essential precaution.

Captain James was informed that in their Lordships' opinion his judgement was at fault in this respect and a notation to this effect should be placed on his record.

A Peters
Naval Secretary

Henry must have felt that after excellent reports throughout his career, Lady Luck had finally deserted him. During his seven months in command of HMS *Capetown*, she had run aground and been torpedoed. The former had resulted in him being advised of 'Their Lordships' displeasure' and the latter had indicated that his 'judgement had been at fault'. If that was not bad enough, his ship was under major repair in Bombay dockyard, where modern ships were being given priority over HMS *Capetown*, by then considered quite an old lady. He knew that even after repairs were completed, she would not be deployed in areas where modern opposition might be expected. In the meantime – and it took over a year to repair her – he had no seagoing command. At forty five years of age he was effectively in limbo.

Soon after Massawa fell into Allied hands, the port became an ammunition depot, serving the East and Mediterranean Fleets. Henry was appointed Naval Officer in Charge of Massawa (Naval Repair Base) for three months until late September 1941, before rejoining HMS *Capetown* in Bombay for three months to oversee, and no doubt endeavour to hasten, repairs and improvements to his ship. The latter included the installation of Type 286 warning radar and six 200 mm Oerlinken Anti-Aircraft guns.

Between 21 December 1941 and 14 February 1942, Henry was appointed Naval Officer i/c Trincomalee, the Naval Station in Ceylon, which maintained and supplied the Fleet. All this chopping and changing of shore stations must have depressed and unsettled Henry. Although there is no evidence to support this assumption, in all probability this was the time when he first contracted tuberculosis, for by late January 1942 Henry was home in England for the first time for four years. He had written to His Majesty the King and received a typically friendly reply. This letter shows that Henry had been unwell and was on sick leave.

By 14 February 1942 Henry had rejoined HMS *Capetown* and after repairs and trials were completed in mid June, according to *Ships Histories* 'from 14th July she was again used for convoy escort duties in the Western Indian Ocean – all without incident or interference.' Between July and November *Ships Movements* record her docking at Khor Kuwai, Pointe Noire, Bombay, Kilindini and Durban.

48. His Majesty's letter to Henry dated 3 February 1942.

Clearly mid 1941 to mid 1942 had been an 'annus horribilis' for Henry. His failing health may have been exacerbated by a drink problem at this stage. Again there is no evidence to support this theory, other than family speculation, but an extract from his Confidential Report, which covered this period, does indicate an uncharacteristic drop in his performance.

17.7.41–17.6.42

Captain James' ship has been undergoing large repairs for the whole of the time he has been under my command.

For a time I appointed him Naval Officer in charge of Trincomalee. This was a time when the place badly needed a good administrator with plenty of drive to organise the defences. Captain James was not happily placed. Making allowance for him being badly understaffed, he did not cooperate well with the Senior Naval Officer afloat or the shore authorities. At Bombay also he did not work in well with the shore authorities. I know Captain James as a sea officer and would expect him to do far better as Commanding Officer of his ship, now that she is in commission. A bachelor. A cheerful manner to his superiors; abrupt to his juniors. Not clever. Plenty of pluck.

Admiral Arbuthnot

17 June 1942

On reflection this report seems a trifle harsh and makes no attempt to understand the circumstances and consequences of Henry's year in limbo. While their Lordships considered that Henry should have deployed one of his sloops to screen HMS *Capetown* from attack from Massawa, the findings of the Board of Enquiry do accept that even if he had done so, the torpedo could still have found its mark. The crew's response and the feat of seamanship in recovering her to Bombay were exemplary and arguably offset Henry's misjudgement, elicited with the benefit of hindsight. The Admiral makes no allowance for Henry's frustration that despite saving her, HMS *Capetown* was given such a low priority in scheduling for repair. Small wonder if he tried and probably failed to persuade the shore authorities to hasten her repair. His remarks about Henry being abrupt with his juniors is strongly countered in a subsequent report, while there is no mention of Henry's sick leave. It is not unreasonable to conclude that Henry found this period exasperating, which in turn affected his health and performance. Serving under a superior officer who appears dismissive did not help.

Between November 1942 and June 1943 Henry was home in the UK undergoing treatment for what was probably the early stages of tuberculosis. In those days TB was a death sentence and was shortly to become a scourge of the post war period. This was before the discovery of the miracle drug streptomycin. It is impossible to decipher all entries in his Record of Service, but it appears he was 'resurveyed' on several occasions during this eight month period. He spent some time in the Royal Naval Hospital Chatham and in a Nursing Home in Aberdeen. He was finally 'surveyed fit for General Service on 6 July 1943' and immediately took over command of HMS *Iron Duke* in Scapa Flow.

July 1943–September 1943. HMS Iron Duke
in command and as Commanding Officer, Auxiliary Patrol Scapa Flow.
Aged 47

(Displacement tonnage 25,000; overall length x breadth 580 x 89.5 ft; top speed 18 knots; complement 580; armament ten 13.5 in, twelve 6 in; HM Dockyard, Portsmouth 12.10.1912.)

Henry was appointed to HMS *Iron Duke* in March 1943, but due to illness, he was not able to report for duty until July. Nevertheless when he did so, he must have recalled that twenty-seven years had elapsed since he had last seen the *Iron Duke*. She had been Admiral Jellicoe's Flagship at the Battle of Jutland in 1916, when Henry had been a midshipman in 'Turret A' in HMS *Collingwood*. In 1931, *Iron Duke* had been converted into a Gunnery Ship and some while later became Headquarters of the Admiral Commanding Orkney & Shetland and acted as an accommodation ship and communications centre off Lyness. Soon after the outbreak of the Second World War in 1939, she was bombed and holed by the Luftwaffe and had to be beached, first at Lyness and subsequently at Longhope. When Henry took over command she was the Base Ship HQ for the Auxiliary Patrol of 71/72 Anti-Submarine Drifter Group, a flotilla of harbour defence MTBs and occasional flotillas of B type Mine Layers. These craft patrolled inside and outside the booms, round the anchorage itself and also the exercise areas.

Throughout both World Wars, Scapa Flow was the Northern base which sheltered ships of the Royal Navy and the Allied Fleets from both storm and enemy attack with sometimes well over 100 vessels lying at anchor. This great harbour is bordered by the mainland, Hoy and South Ronaldsay.

Between September and November 1943 Henry commanded HMS *Proserpine*, a shore station or stone frigate, nicknamed 'Proper Swine.' As well as commanding this Minesweeper & Anti Submarine Base Depot, he was Maintenance Captain, Orkneys and Shetlands. At the conclusion of his five month tour in Scapa Flow, he received a good but revealing report:

An average officer as regards leadership, influence and personality – loyal and tactful – sound common sense. Good manner with subordinates. Excellent social qualities. Passed physically fit. While this officer has carried out his duties as Commanding Officer *Iron Duke* and

Maintenance Captain to my complete satisfaction, I am doubtful if he is
equal to the strain of a seagoing command.
Admiral Wells
5 December 1943

While Henry had succeeded remarkably well in both commands after his
illness, this report effectively prevented him being appointed to any future
seagoing command. His lack of robust health prescribed this.

January 1944–February 1945. HMS Squid
in Command. Aged 48

Nevertheless his next appointment commanding HMS *Squid*, a shore station
in Southampton, demanded both the stamina and skills of a Naval
Operations Staff Officer in the build up to the invasion of North West Europe.
In June 1942 HMS *Squid* had been established as a Tank Landing Craft Repair
Base at Messrs Harland & Wolff B works in Southampton Docks. Shortly
after Henry's arrival the Royal Navy commandeered the Westcliffe Hall
Hotel, Hythe to accommodate the Squadron Staff required to plan the alloca-
tion and assembly of Landing Craft for invasion Forces G and J. Although
Top Secret at the time, on D Day these Forces were destined for the assault
landings in Normandy – Force G to 'Gold' and Force J to 'Sword' beaches.

Henry, like hundreds of thousands of other Allied Troops taking part in
'Operation Overlord', must have been galvanised in to superhuman effort
by the excitement of the build up to D Day in the South of England. Henry
and HMS *Squid* Squadron Staff worked all hours to ensure that the arrangements for the assembly of Forces G and J went like clockwork. He must
have been thrilled to be directly involved in 'Operation Neptune', the
counterpart Codeword used by the Navy for the same operation.

Amassing all the necessary ships and landing craft to their respective
ports of embarkation required an unprecedented master plan. At one stage
the shortage of landing craft seemed critical until the shortfall arrived from
other theatres of operation, particularly from the Italian Campaign. The
issuing of naval orders alone called for several thousand workers. The
systematic reception, briefing, ferrying and embarkation of assault troops
were massive operations. Each vessel was given a numbered position in its
convoy, a steaming speed and a position to ride at anchor on arrival in the
Bay of the Seine before H Hour for the assault landing. While many sailors
and soldiers had previous experience of assault landings on a smaller scale,
this was a 5,000 vessel fleet operation and the greatest logistical shipping
movement ever attempted. Moreover, to achieve surprise, it had to be done
without breaking radio silence.

Like so many others who saw Forces G and J leave their anchorage in the Solent and head for France early on the 5 June 1944, Henry will have been humbled by the sheer size of this combined operation and just relieved that the assembly and launch had gone well. As they witnessed the fleet of landing craft, together with their air and naval escort, disappear from view, all prayed for a successful Allied Invasion of the Normandy beaches.[20]

Gradually as encouraging radio bulletins emerged during the remainder of June, a feeling of relief will have been felt by everyone at home and particularly by those who had taken part, but had been left behind. It was during this time of anti climax that Henry was to hear that his younger brother, John had been killed in action near Lake Trasimene in Italy on 26 June. This must have brought back memories of Eric in 1916. Henry was now the sole survivor of three brothers in arms.

Within months the experience gained by HMS *Squid* in preparing for D Day, was once again put into practice. This infinitely smaller operation, codenamed 'Infatuate', involved a ground attack by British and Canadian forces being launched to seize the Island of Walcheren in the Scheldt estuary. This was designed to open the port of Antwerp for Naval Convoys to supply the advancing Allied Armies. The island was defended by

Photograph courtesy of the Imperial War Museum, London

49. Force G landing craft at Southampton, 1 June 1944.

German 70th Infantry Division, which barred the approach to Antwerp with its coastal batteries. After the island had been shelled by the Battleship *Warspite* and the monitors *Erebus* and *Roberts*, 152 Brigade, 4th Commando and the 4th Special Service Brigade launched their assault on 1 November 1944. After determined German resistance during which 26 landing craft were lost and subsequent extensive demolitions of the port, the German Garrison finally surrendered eight days later. After major repairs to the port, the first Allied Convoy entered Antwerp on 1 December.

Naval Records show that three officers from HMS *Squid* were awarded the Distinguished Service Cross for their services at Sword Beach during the Normandy Landing in June 1944 and during the assault on Walcheren in November 1944. When Henry handed over command of HMS *Squid* on the 19 February 1945, he received a large brass ash tray from his Squadron and two letters of commendation relating to his part in preparations for D Day:

Admiralty
17 February 1945

I am commanded by my Lords Commissioners of the Admiralty to inform you that they have had before them, a report of your good services in the planning and execution of the operations for the invasion of Normandy, and I am to say that their Lordships have noted with satisfaction the part you played in this great enterprise.
I am Sir
Your obedient servant
HB Markham

No A25
26 February 1945

This is to certify that Captain PHG James Royal Navy has served as Commanding Officer in HMS Squid under my command from 12th day of January 1944 to the 19th day of February 1945 during which period he has conducted himself entirely to my satisfaction.
An able and enthusiastic and extremely energetic Commanding Officer of HMS Squid he was responsible for the arrangements of the assembly of Forces G and J in Southampton area for the preparation and operation of the hards and the administration of the craft running the Shuttle Service in the area.
All these tasks he has carried out with marked success.
FA Buckley
Commodore
Landing Craft Bases, Portsmouth

Photograph courtesy of the Imperial War Museum, London

50. Landing craft loaded on to transporters at Nijmegen.

February 1945–April 1945. Naval Commander, Force U Crossing the Rhine

As the Allies fought their way towards Germany it became clear that crossing the Rhine posed a serious obstacle for the Army. This was largely because the engines of the Army's usual craft were not strong enough for the Rhine current which, opposite Rees, was about four knots. Montgomery turned to the Royal Navy for help. A small group of Naval Officers from Combined Operations at the Admiralty took three weeks to plan, train, organise and deploy a Naval Force inland capable of constructing pontoon bridges across the Rhine to launch the Army into Germany without loosing momentum.

Bearing in mind Henry's experience of coordinating flotillas of Landing Craft for D Day and Walcheren, it is hardly surprising that he was chosen to command the British Naval Units of Force U being deployed to enable 21st Army Group to cross the Rhine.

Two days after leaving HMS *Squid* on 19 February, Henry attended an Eastern Landing Craft Base Committee meeting. This was to coordinate the final stages of bringing together six flotillas of landing craft and 1200 men from Portsmouth and Tilbury to Antwerp and Ostend on 23 and 24 February for 'Operation Banknote.' The Army then provided convoys of ten wheeled trucks to carry the landing craft and sailors overland across Dutch roads for more than 100 miles to selected crossing points.

On 1 April 1945, and for the first time in Naval History, the White Ensign flew over HMS *Landseer*, the name of the Naval Base on the Rhine. The nerve

Photograph courtesy of the Imperial War Museum, London

51. Landing craft being unloaded on the banks of the Rhine.

centre for the Naval Force was MOLCAB (Mobile Landing Craft Advanced Base), which was established to maintain and supply three subsidiary landing craft bases on the river, all self supporting units working together to keep the amphibious force operating effectively.

Photograph courtesy of the Imperial War Museum, London

52. Naval landing craft form the first completed bridge in the British sector, 1945.

An extract from *Sunday Times* 25 March 1945 paints the scene:

NAVY FOUND NEW WAY FOR INLAND WAR
RIVER TECHNIQUE

S.H.A.E.F., Saturday

In transferring swarms of men and vast quantities of material across the swiftly flowing and broad waters of the Rhine an entirely new amphibious technique was necessary.

Months ago it was apparent that the armies would need a ferry service across the river once the bridgeheads were established and before bridges could be thrown across. A fast service of craft strong enough to carry tanks, bulldozers and mobile guns safely over was required and LCMs (Landing Craft Mechanised) and LCVPs (Landing Craft, Vehicle, Personnel) were found to meet these needs.

Crews were trained in French and Belgian waters to manoeuvre the craft to and from pinpoint landing spots in strong currents and to launch them from muddy river banks. Many of these craft measuring 77 ft in length, 14 ft in width and nearly 25 ft high were moved to their launching sites over roads pitted with shell holes and over makeshift bridges and through narrow village streets.

Both types of craft have bows which lower to form ramps for loading and unloading, thus making unnecessary any mechanical loading devices. They can supply a beachhead with vital materials for its defence while the enemy is still off balance and while other means of spanning the river are in progress.

SOLDIER–SAILORS

During their months of training naval officers and men lived and worked exactly as soldiers. Completely to disguise their presence they wore Army uniforms and helmets, covering or completely discarding all naval insignia.

The operations were under the direction of the Allied Naval Commander-in-Chief of the Expeditionary Force. United States Navy units were under general command of Vice Admiral Alan G Kirk, Commanding United States Naval Forces in France. The senior officer of the British Naval Units was Captain P H G James, RN and Cmdr William J Whiteside, United States Navy, was in charge of the United States Units.

A detailed training programme similar to that for D Day was drawn up for the amphibious operation, and huge numbers of photographs were taken from the air. Over 1,000,000 such photographs were taken in preparation for the airborne operation alone. A hundred thousand tons of ammunition were brought up to the British Second Army.

Reuter and Exchange.

Photograph courtesy of the Imperial War Museum, London

53. Henry and his Staff study a map of the Rhine battle area at the base.
The official caption to this photograph is:
BRITISH NAVAL BASE IN GERMANY. 25 MARCH 1945, IN THE REICHSWALD
FOREST. A ROYAL NAVY "MOLCAB" - MOBILE LANDING CRAFT ADVANCED
BASE, NEAR THE RHINE. THE FORCE UNDER THE COMMAND OF CAPTAIN
P H G JAMES, RN, ARE PATROLLING AND BRIDGE BUILDING ALONG THE
RHINE AND HAVE BROUGHT PRISONERS ACROSS TO THE WESTERN SHORE.
ALL PERSONNEL LIVE UNDER CANVAS IN THE FOREST AND THE CAMP IS
ADMINISTERED AND RUN BY ROYAL MARINES.
Left to right: Lieut Cdr R G A Verity, RNVR; Capt P H G James, RN;
Capt J Lemasurier, RM; Lieut R E Whittaker, RM, studying a map of the Rhine
battle area at the base.

The successful amphibious crossing of the Rhine enabled 21st Army Group
to press forward without losing momentum with this great river to their
rear. Moreover several unblown bridges and the many landing craft
available helped to convert a former serious obstacle into an essential
supply line. This meant that the role of Force U had changed from amphibious assault to supply, requiring differing skills and a reduced team.

Many of Force U Naval Party 1756, including its Commander, were
posted elsewhere. In Henry' case he was posted in April for two months to
HMS *Odyssey*[21] on the staff of ANCXF (Allied Naval Commander
Expeditionary Force), and in command of Eclipse Transit and Assembly
Area.

Victory in Europe

At long last after further bitter fighting, the German Army surrendered on 8 May 1945 on Lüneberg Heath to Eisenhower and Montgomery. Henry, whose forty ninth birthday came four days later, had made an important contribution to the Rhine crossing. In retrospect, it is a little surprising that he did not receive an award for his services.

June 1945–January 1946. HMS Stag
Senior Naval Officer, Red Sea and Canal Area. Aged 49

It is reasonable to assume that Henry's next posting turned on past experience and health considerations. Between 1940 and 1942, when commanding HMS *Capetown* he had learnt much about the Aden and Massawa region, while he knew the port of Alexandria and the Suez Canal from earlier naval cruises of the Mediterranean. The Red Sea climate was probably considered helpful to Henry's suspect health and got him out of England during the winter of 1945.

HMS *Stag* was a Shore Station in Port Said and an independent command. After the end of the War, Port Said at the northerly end of the Suez Canal, was considered a strategic post in the Middle East, which still demanded a Royal Naval presence. While former enemies licked their wounds after nearly six years of hostilities, Henry's next six months service appears to have been without incident and mainly routine.

Unfortunately on the 5 February 1946 Henry's health broke down once more and he was admitted to the Royal Naval Hospital, Chatham with tuberculosis for a period of eighteen months. Ultimately, in August 1947, one month after he had been appointed ADC to the King, he was discharged to his home. Six months later on 12 January 1948, aged fifty one and after thirty four years service he was medically discharged. Unlike his two brothers Eric and John, he had survived both World Wars but had retired in poor health. He must have missed the camaraderie of his service life and have found civilian life rather lonely. He will have welcomed visits from former colleagues and have enjoyed reminiscing over times past. Nevertheless after a lifetime of distinguished and loyal service to King and Country, this final chapter of his life, in failing health and mostly on his own, may have been tinged with sadness. On reflection being a Captain at the age of 43 at the outbreak of the Second World War in September 1939, made Henry well placed for further promotion during his next five and a half years of war service. However this did not happen and it is natural enough to ask why? With hindsight it seems to have been that a combination of events and circumstances appeared to work against him.

54. Captain P. Henry Gwynne-James RN

There was the evidence of some poor judgement and bad luck relating to HMS *Capetown* running aground in the Nicobar Islands and soon afterwards in April 1941 being torpedoed off Massawa. Nevertheless this was offset by the excellent response of his ship's company and the subsequent long and successful recovery of his ship to Bombay.

The latter resulted in him being penalised by receiving a series of shore postings while HMS *Capetown* due to her age was given low priority repair in Bombay Dockyard. Unfortunately he seemed unable to contain his frustration at this protracted delay at a critical stage in the war at sea. In all probability he sought solace in alcohol which affected his performance during understaffed shore postings in hot climates, where health and hygiene were at a premium.

It is likely that Henry contracted tuberculosis during his three months in Trincomalee and the onset of this wretched disease, which may not have been diagnosed immediately, must have filled him with despair. This and his drinking made matters worse and caused a sharp deterioration in his relationship with both his seniors and subordinates.

By the time he was commanding HMS *Capetown* again at sea in February 1942, his ship was perceived as a dated cruiser which needed to be shaded from operations against more modern higher specification enemy ships.

Although his three month command of HMS *Iron Duke* at Scapa Flow in 1943 was successful, he was not considered sufficiently robust in health for a seagoing command thereafter. Generally speaking command at sea during wartime is where promotion is won.

To his great credit when he must have been disappointed by this turn of events, he applied his operational staff skills with energy while commanding HMS *Squid* during landing craft preparations for D day at Southampton and when commanding the British Naval task force for the Rhine crossing.

Appendices

Appendix 1   Statement of Service
Appendix 2   Extract from The Westminster Gazette, January 16, 1913, and
             Telegram from HRH Prince Albert to Henry arranging to meet
             to go by train together to Plymouth.
Appendix 3   Extracts from Henry's report on the torpedoing of
             HMS *Capetown* off Massawa on 8 April 1941

Appendix 1
Statement of Service
Captain P H G James Royal Navy

15 September 1913	Midshipman
15 September 1915	Acting Sub Lieutenant
15 May 1916	Sub Lieutenant
15 September 1917	Acting Lieutenant
15 November 1917	Lieutenant
15 November 1925	Lieutenant Commander
31 December 1931	Commander
31 June 1938	Captain
12 January 1948	Retired (Medically Unfit)

As Midshipman, Acting Sub Lieutenant and Sub Lieutenant

1913–1915	HMS *Collingwood*
1916 (3 weeks)	HMS *Foxglove*
1916–1917	HMS *Collingwood*

As Acting Lieutenant

1917–1919	HMS *Redoubt*

As Lieutenant

1919–1921	HMS *Temeraire*
1921–1922	HMS *Colleen*
1922–1923	HMS *Vancouver*
1924–1925	HMS *Versatile*
1925–1925	HMS *Shakespeare*

As Lieutenant Commander

1925–1929	HMS *Stormcloud*
1929–1932	HMS *Antelope*

As Commander

1932–1933	HMS *Pembroke*
1933–1936	Ministry of Defence as Director of Personal Services
1936–1938	HMS *Fearless*
1938 (6 months)	Ministry of Defence with Operations Division, Naval Staff

Captain

September 1938 – October 1938	HMS *Mackay*
October 1938 – October 1940	Naval Liaison Officer, Shanghai
November 1940 – June 1941	HMS *Capetown* in Command
July 1941 – September 1941	Naval Officer in Charge, Massawa (Naval Repair Base)
September 1941 – December 1941	HMS *Capetown* in Command
December 1941 – February 1942	Naval Officer in Charge, Trincomalee, Ceylon
March 1942 – November 1942	HMS *Capetown* in Command
November 1942 – June 1943	On sick leave in UK
March 1943 – September 1943	HMS *Iron Duke* in Command and as Commanding Officer, Auxiliary Patrol, Scapa Flow
September 1943 – November 1943	HMS *Proserpine* additional as Maintenance Captain, Orkneys and Shetlands
January 1944 – February 1945	HMS *Squid* in Command (Operation Neptune – Normandy)
February 1945 – April 1945	Naval Commander, Force 'U'(Rhine Crossing)
April 1945 – May 1945	HMS *Odyssey* on staff of ANCXF, and in Command of Eclipse Transit and Assembly Area
June 1945 – January 1946	HMS *Stag* additional and as Senior Naval Officer, Red Sea and Canal area
February 1946 – August 1947	Royal Naval Hospital Chatham. Tuberculosis
August 1947 – December 1947	On sick leave at home.
12 January 1948	Retired. Medically unfit

Appendix 2

**Extract from The Westminster Gazette, 16 January 1913;
and Telegram from HRH Prince Albert to Henry
arranging to meet to go by train together to Plymouth.**

THE WESTMINSTER GAZETTE. JANUARY 16, 1913

THE KING'S SECOND SON.

Prince Albert Victor, second son of the King, with seventy other naval cadets, just passed out from Dartmouth Naval College, will join the "Cumberland" sea-going training ship at Devonport to-morrow afternoon for a cruise to the Canary Islands and the West Indies and back. The Prince will be away about six months. The "Cumberland" sails on Saturday afternoon.

POST OFFICE TELEGRAPHS.

Sandringham

TO { H. James aylestone Hill Stukeford

am leaving by 11 am train from Paddington friday can you come to Buckingham Palace at 10.15 am if not meet at Bookstall under the clock at Paddington albert.

Appendix 3

Extracts from Henry's report on the torpedoing of HMS *Capetown* off Massawa on 8 April 1941

1st May, 1941.

No. 1410/18.

THE TORPEDOING OF H.M.S. CAPETOWN
OFF KUBA, ERITREA, AT 0215 (ZONE -3) ON 8TH APRIL,
1941, BY AN ENEMY 'E' BOAT

Sir,

I have the honour to forward the following detailed report concerning the torpedoing of CAPETOWN off Kuba, Eritrea (Lat: 16° 11' 30" North, Long: 59 13' East), at 0215 (zone -3) on 8th April, 1941, by an enemy 'E' boat.

2.   The report is necessarily incomplete consequent on the fact that 'B' boiler room is still flooded with water. It was hoped while at Port Sudan that it would have been possible to fit a patch over the hole and thus enable the interior of 'B' boiler room to be thoroughly examined. This, however, was not possible. It is for this reason that it has been impossible up to the present time accurately to answer all the questions asked by the relevant Confidential Admiralty Fleet Orders.
This report has therefore not been addressed to VERNON and the individual Admiralty departments. I am however, forwarding the ormig master of this report in order that copies may be forwarded to these authorities should you think fit.

3.   I have made the report as detailed as possible in order that others (particularly those serving in ships of the same class) may gain by the experiences of those serving in CAPETOWN.
In this connection, I would like to state that officers and men of CAPETOWN have taken full advantage of other warship's experiences - such as the damage suffered during the River Plate action, the sinking of CALYPSO, etc.,

4.   It has been the practice in CAPETOWN to exercise frequently action stations at which breakdowns and damage were always the major subject, as opposed to the ordinary action stations, such as those before dawn and at dusk, and those purely to exercise the control, etc. These have purposely always been short (no longer than ½ hour) in order to avoid staleness and boredom; always "high speed" ones as regards happenings that one might expect in any action - a bomb here, a near-miss there, a torpedo, fire, etc. - all of which cause a certain amount of damage to various parts of the ship, which immediately require the correct action on the part of the officers and ship's company to keep the ship in fighting trim.

These action stations

13.   Accordingly, I decided to conserve the oil fuel of INDUS and PARRAMATTA so that I should not find myself at the critical moment (i.e. when Massawa had fallen and the opening of sea communications with it were vitally important) with both my minesweepers (INDUS and PARRAMATTA) having to proceed to Port Sudan to fuel.

14.   I therefore directed both of them to anchor to seaward of Meres Kuba and remain at short notice for steam during the night.

15.   CAPETOWN was patrolling to seaward of INDUS and PARRAMATTA and within the area which had previously been swept off the anchorage.

Weather and sea conditions during the night 7th/8th April.

16.   Wind - calm.
       Sea and swell - 11.
       Sky - b7.
       Moon - ⅝ full (bearing 275°, elevation 15°, setting).
       Horizon to seaward - dark and therefore extremely difficult to sight a small target.

21.   I myself was resting fully clothed in a deck chair within four yards of the compass platform, and was just due for one of my periodical night calls.

Behaviour of CAPETOWN at moment of impact.

22.   The torpedo hit the ship in the centre of 'B' boiler room on the starboard side.
       'B' boiler room was completely flooded in 15 seconds and the ship heeled over approximately ten or twelve degrees to starboard, immediately rolling back again to about seven degrees to port, and then settled on a list of two and a half degrees to starboard.

23.   The explosion threw up a large column of water which enveloped the greater part of the ship and also produced a wave along the starboard waist.

24.   All main and auxiliary machinery stopped within approximately one minute of the explosion. The dynamos having stopped, all electric lighting failed.

Immediate steps taken on the bridge.

25.   An extremely short time elapsed between the moment the torpedo hit the ship and the receipt by me on the bridge of the report of the actual state of affairs from the Damage Control Officer. The report was - "'B' boiler room holed and flooded. Bulkheads holding and being shored."

55.   An inspection was made along the whole of the lower deck to ensure that all watertight doors, hatches and valves were shut and that none had been overlooked. Furthermore, all oil tanks and spaces were sounded. (excepting those between 'B' boiler room bulkheads).

56.   Well within an hour of the explosion, there were eight most essential shores placed between both boilers in 'A' boiler room and No.91 bulkhead (i.e. the forward bulkhead of 'B' boiler room). There were also six shores fixed against the after side of the after bulkhead of 'B' boiler room and two fixed on the forward bulkhead of the forward engine room. The hatches to 'B' boiler room air lock, No.3 magazine and shell room were also shored. The speed with which this operation was carried out was in a great part due to constant practices having been previously carried out and the fact that these essential shores had already been cut to the requisite length and stored in accessible positions well known to the personnel concerned.

57.   The organisation worked smoothly and faultlessly throughout. The courage and determination shown by everyone concerned was exemplary.

Family Recollections

Henry was of small, neat stature with hair swept straight back, immaculately dressed and with a dapper presence which seemed to invite respect. He had a rather aquiline face with typical pronounced James nose and sharp discerning eyes. His fairly stern countenance would crease into a happy and infectious smile.

Harold's elder daughter and my cousin, Margaret, who was also Henry's goddaughter, recalls a revealing incident involving her Uncle Henry while staying with her Granny James and her Aunty Trill at Tidnacott in the late 1920's. `I can remember Uncle Henry teaching me to make a cat's cradle with a ball of Granny's knitting wool. We were sitting at the round table in the bay window in the dining room when Uncle Henry spied Miss Taggart approaching the side door. To my amazement he suddenly hid himself behind one of the long curtains covering the window seat. Then when Miss Taggart was talking to Aunty Trill in the hall, he climbed out through the window and remained in the garden while we all had our tea at the round table. I can't think who Miss Taggart was or where she came from, but she always arrived on foot. My own father also shot off whenever she dropped in!

By the late 1940s when Davina and I got to know him, he was not robust of health and we were aware of some care with his breathing. Although

I remember being a little disappointed that he was not a genuine sports enthusiast, he seemed to approve of all Davina and I were up to and occasionally spoke of our father (his younger brother) with great affection.

He had a ready sense of humour and was the instigator of our holiday visits to London to lunch with our Great Aunt Lena (Lady Baillie). This was followed by the reward of either attending a matinée of a top musical (*Oklahoma, Carousel, Annie Get Your Gun*) or occasionally tea at the Ritz.

He enjoyed hatching this plan, realising full well how we all (including our mother) lived in awe of Auntie Lena, who showed great interest in our general knowledge about current affairs and our academic progress at our respective schools. Quite often lunch was taken at Bailley's Hotel where Auntie Lena would demand her usual table and expect instant service.

We recall on one occasion that there was undue delay in the usual prompt service and she rounded on Uncle Henry, 'Surely you would not accept this on the bridge of HMS *Fearless*, Hennie?' Thus our Uncle was dispatched, much to our embarrassment, to find the Head Waiter to summon him personally to take our order. Davina and I were appalled that a former Captain of many of Her Majesty's Ships should have been sent scuttling off by a woman in this way. In retrospect, he was probably not best pleased either, but to have declined to do so could have caused a family scene in front of the children.

As mentioned this holiday high spot consisted of a delicious but daunting luncheon with Auntie Lena and Uncle Henry. This required our best table manners and good answers to searching questions from Auntie Lena on current affairs. Indeed during the preceeding weeks our mother had encouraged us to read the papers and listen to the radio as if preparing for an exam. We shared out likely topics between us, tested one another mercilessly and were seldom caught out. Sometimes it was important to curb the enthusiasm of our answers. Was it a game that Auntie Lena played along with? We shall never know.

Keeping a surreptitious eye on our watches, the time came for Uncle Henry to pay the bill and hail a taxi to convey us all back to 23 Queen's Gate Gardens. After taking the lift to her flat we all thanked her, kissed her and bade her goodbye. We soon emerged from the lift at ground floor, wreathed in smiles and began to savour the excitement of going to a musical with Uncle Henry.

In common with all those fortunate enough to see these exhilarating and romantic big stage American musicals at that time, we were transfixed with delight. After the deprivations of six years at war – defeats, black-outs, air raids, rationing, loss of life, victories and economic decline – here at last was a musical declaration of unbridled happiness and toe tapping confidence in the future.

After the show Uncle Henry would accompany two enwrapped children and their mother by taxi to Waterloo Station. He would see us off on the Farnham train waving our goodbyes with our treasured programmes. We felt a little sad for him returning alone to his bachelor flat at 64 Lowlands Road at Harrow-on-the-Hill.

Davina and I detected that our mother was fond of Henry and together they had enjoyed plotting these regular school holiday outings to London. We were all grateful to him for his generosity in arranging and paying for everything. Such an expense was by then far beyond our Mother's budget. It was a kind of return to pre-war times at Aylestone Hill, Hereford when much fun was had by all the family. In those days our Grandmother (known by us as 'Granny Hereford') had been the benevolent matriarch.

In due course failing health caused Henry to leave Harrow-on-the Hill in London and return to Hereford where Mary, his eldest sister cared for him at Danesmere. They had always been devoted to each other ever since Mary had helped him with his studies for entrance into the Royal Navy. During this happy final chapter of his life, he enjoyed frequent visits to Highcroft near Breinton, Hereford, the lovely home of his younger brother Philip and his wife Grace and their three young daughters, Philippa, Caro and Anna.

My cousin, Caro recalls 'a very much loved uncle who we knew well when he moved back to Hereford. Our parents loved having him to stay and there was always much laughter. He would take a long time getting dressed due to his breathlessness and eventually would come down to breakfast and appear at the door asking "What's the drill for today, Grace?" He called the floor "the deck" as though he was still on board ship, which amused us all.'

My cousin, Anna remembers 'Henry's sense of fun showed up when having a family supper with us all. After my bath I flounced downstairs pretending to be a posh lady – a towel wrapped round me – seeing Henry sitting at the table I turned round and fled in shyness revealing a bare behind. Everyone collapsed with laughter – especially Uncle Henry, who wept with delight!'

As Henry's health deteriorated further, Mary had a lift installed at Danesmere to help Henry 'go aloft to his cabin.' He died on 10 August 1959, aged sixty three.

CHAPTER 4

John Gwynne-James
1903-1944

Early Life

Quite recently I was told by an experienced journalist that writing about one's own father is seldom successful due to filial influence which renders a balanced account so difficult to achieve. However when he heard the circumstances in my case he did admit the general rule might not apply. These are, that at the age of sixty seven, I am writing about a man whom I last saw when I was about five years old and who was killed when he was only forty, nearly sixty years ago. I shall bear in mind the journalist's warning and but press forward in the knowledge that in my case there are so few left who remember him. I shall leave it to those select few to decide whether the journalist was right or not. Other readers may wish to draw their own conclusions.

John and his sister Trill, who were the second pair of twins and the youngest members of the family, were born on 16 September 1903. All eight children were fortunate to be brought up in the family home at Aylestone Hill in Hereford. Their father Frank was the third generation to head the family firm Gwynne-James & Sons, Solicitors and had been Mayor of Hereford in 1898. Their mother Sophie, a remarkably fine looking woman ran the family home like clockwork yet managed to make time for charities like the Waifs & Strays, for painting seascapes of her native North Cornwall and for playing her accordion. The James family invariably joined Sophie's parents, the Waddon Martyns at Tonacombe Manor, near Morwenstowe in North Cornwall for their Summer Holidays. These were spent in the nearby holiday cottage, Tidnacott which had outstanding views over the cliffs to the sea. It must have been a very happy and exhilarating childhood.

In 1911 John followed Eric to Moorland House Preparatory School at Cheswall in Cheshire. During his five years at Moorland House John's ambition was to follow Henry into the Royal Navy. However to his great disappointment he failed the eye test due to slight colour blindness. In late October 1916 soon after his thirteenth birthday he heard the wretched news that Eric had died of wounds in France.

In 1917 John became the seventh member of the family to go to Cheltenham College and boarded at Newick House. In those days boys were expected to choose either Classical or Military Studies and when they left College the majority pursued careers in either the Church, the Diplomatic or in the Armed Services. By then it is likely that John had made up his mind to follow Eric into the Army and also to join the King's Shropshire Light Infantry. Unlike Eric he had no aspirations to go to University, but like so many of his contemporaries had set his sights on going to the Royal Military College, Sandhurst to gain a Commission in the Regular Army. Like Eric he played for College at both Rugby and Cricket. He played full back for College 1st XV in 1921 and was reputedly a fearless tackler. In the same year he was in the same College Cricket XI as K S Duleepsinhji (later of Cambridge University, Sussex CCC and England), who helped win many school matches with his remarkable eye and languid style. John's role was fast round arm bowler which invited some criticism from the purists. When batting during the Cheltenham v Haileybury match at Lord's in 1921 he hit a huge six which struck the clock face below Father Time.[22]

After passing the Civil Service (Army) Entrance Examination he left Cheltenham College in July 1921 and started his two year course at the RMC Sandhurst in September. He played cricket for the Sandhurst 1st XI which beat the RMA Woolwich at Lord's during his final summer and was commissioned into The King's Shropshire Light infantry in August 1923.

55. John batting at RMC Sandhurst, August 1923.

56. John in civilian clothes wearing an Old Cheltonian tie.

57. John with his mother at Aylestone Hill, 1927

58. Jalapahar in Bengal, where John met Anne on 28 May 1928.

59. Anne at Clovelly, August 1929.

60. John and Anne at Tidnacott, August 1929.
61. John carrying June, his niece at Aylestone Hill, 1929.

62. John with Biddy, July 1930.

63. John with his mother at Aylestone Hill, July 1931.

64. Anne on her engagement to John in 1933.

Pre War Service

During the next ten years John served with the 1st Battalion KSLI in India while they were stationed in Poona, Dinapore, Razmak and Gharial. As is evident from his Statement of Service at Appendix 1, this was a period of active soldiering on the North West Frontier, either on the Plains or in the Hills, and attending various Support Weapon Training Courses. This was interspersed with local leave in the cooler climate of various hill stations and occasional home leave starting and ending with long sea voyages home to England and back.

Indian Summers demanded that, other than when on exercise, camp routine consisted of a very early start to the day's training followed by early afternoon siesta. Then there would be a variety of active sport and recreation laid on within and between regiments for the remainder of the day. Of an evening there was often some form of entertainment or social event. Many of these would be organised by the Officers' or Sergeants' Messes or in conjunction with local Indian Civil Service communities. Invitations to the Theatre, Hunt Balls, Government House Garden Parties and Tiger

Shooting were much sought after. Much has since been written about this period, often referred to as The Last of the British Raj.

As far as John was concerned this must have been a marvellous introduction to soldiering. He was serving with a first class regiment where he made longstanding friendships. Many of his brother officers were outstanding sportsmen and his love of sport led to a full and very active life. As well as playing cricket, rugby and hockey he was able to play polo, to shoot and referee Boxing Championships. At the time the KSLI had an outstanding Hockey XI which included three Irish Hockey Internationals. During this ten year period, they won the Army Cup on eight occasions and were runners up in the other two. John, who played back, was christened 'the tank' for his robust tackling.

To cap it all, while in Jalapahar, just above Darjeeling, John met Anne, who was to become the love of his life. However, this was not straight forward as Anne was already married, but in the throes of seeking a divorce from an officer in the Royal Engineers. John's posting to the Regimental Depot at Shrewsbury between 1929 and 1931, ensured that they both had the opportunity to meet each other's families and plan their future together. In October 1931 John rejoined the 1st Battalion at Gharial in India and a year later was posted home to the 2nd Battalion in Colchester. At long last, after waiting five years for Anne's divorce to be granted, they were married at Salisbury Registry Office on 19 December 1933. They spent their honeymoon at Tidnacott.

During John's eighteen months as Staff Captain, 11th Infantry Brigade in Colchester, Davina was born on 25 September 1934. In April 1935 he returned to the 2nd Battalion just up the road in Colchester and later took over as Adjutant for their move to Pembroke Dock in July 1935. He was an outstanding Adjutant for the next three and a half years during the regiment's happy and successful tour in South Wales. On 12 June 1937 I was born.

As a loving husband and father of two young children, and like all others similarly blessed, he was immensely proud of his family. This pride is on record in the three books of cuttings which he kept. The first was of the letters and presents received on his marriage to Anne, fairly standard practice then and now. The next two books were of congratulatory letters received when Davina and I were born. Again most families did and still do the same. What is perhaps a little unusual is that this was entirely done by him and in both our cases included a detailed weekly weight record for the first year compared with Trufood's 'average' baby and also a record of vaccinations. It had an events page which recorded house moves, christenings and later progress reports on our cutting of teeth, increasing mobility and height. While our mother's handwriting shows that she

65. Anne carrying Davina in Colchester days.

66. John with Davina and David in the garden at Littlegates.

continued these records when the war took John away, it does show his real concern for our health and development.

By the time John handed over to his successor as Adjutant in December 1938 and became Staff Captain to 3rd Infantry Brigade in Bordon, Hampshire in January 1939, the deepening threat of yet another war with Germany was uppermost in most people's minds. It was during this period that John and Anne rented Littlegates, a delightful cottage off the Tilford Road near Farnham in Surrey. This was destined to become our family home for many years to come.

Second World War

While the first fifteen years of John's service had been relatively typical of the time, the next five changed tempo dramatically after the declaration of war in September 1939. Within the next four years he was destined to be promoted from Staff Captain to Brigade Commander of 3rd Infantry Brigade. A closer look at his remarkable wartime service will perhaps throw some light on why he was so successful.

Soon after the outbreak of hostilities on 24 September 1939 he embarked for France with 3rd Infantry Brigade only to return two months later to attend a Short Course at the Staff College in Camberley. Normally this Course would have been a year but because the war was well under way and time was of the essence, it was compressed into three months. The Students, some of whom, like John, had failed the Staff College Exam, still attended due to their excellent service record and strong recommendation.[23] Many may have wished to be elsewhere but there was plenty of incentive to learn from highly experienced Directing Staff and then to return to do battle with the enemy.

On completing the Course on 20 April 1940 and probably much to his delight, he was appointed General Staff Officer Grade 3 to 4th Division and embarked for France on 27 May to rejoin the British Expeditionary Force. BBC news bulletins reported the plight of the BEF during their withdrawal towards Dunkirk. But these were expurgated versions of a confused and

Camarades!

Telle est la situation!
En tout cas, la guerre est finie pour vous!
    Vos chefs vont s'enfuir par avion.
A bas les armes!

British Soldiers!

Look at this map: it gives your true situation!
Your troops are entirely surrounded —
    stop fighting!
Put down your arms!

67. Propaganda leaflet dropped by German aircraft in May 1940.

often chaotic situation. John must have wondered what to expect and where he would find 4th Division Headquarters.

The logic of his posting soon evaporated for he had arrived in France on the second day of Operation Dynamo, the miraculous nine day evacuation of 366,162 British and French troops from Dunkirk between 26 May and 3 June 1940. The situation was grave indeed. Boulogne had fallen on 24 May, Calais on 26 May and on 27 May the Belgian army had surrendered, opening up the left flank. Meanwhile the Germans tried to break through the perimeter defences and had bombed Dunkirk port out of action. The BEF and the First French Army were retreating into the perimeter of Dunkirk and the Royal Navy, under the direction of the Senior Naval Officer, Captain W G Tennant CB MVO RN, were beginning to ferry troops in boats from the beach to ships anchored in the channel off shore. The Germans had bombed the waterworks which supplied Dunkirk and had put out of action any aerodrome north of Abbeville. While the latter did not affect Bomber Command, RAF fighter sorties over France were restricted to about fifteen minutes due to their limited range. Despite gallant intercepts by RAF fighters, accounting for 377 enemy at a cost of 87 own aircraft within nine days, the Germans continued to bomb the Allied enclave day and night. Beneath were 350,000 men with all their possessions within a narrow compass. Perfect targets included columns crowded on roads, shipping crowded in a channel and masses of men upon the beach. The only consolations were that the smoke from burning oil tanks often hampered bomb aiming and those dropped on the beach sometimes penetrated deep into the sand before exploding.

After some confusion as to what he should now do, John was appointed Assistant Brigade Major to Beauman Division, often referred to as 'Beau Force'. This was a group which had been formed from a mix of isolated and detached units to help delay the German Army so as to allow the bulk of the British and French Armies to evacuate from Dunkirk beach. Such had been the success of the German Army's blitzkreig tactics, this gallant rearguard was crucial. While the 1st Battalion KSLI, which he would later command, was the last British regiment to leave Dunkirk on 2 June, John's service record shows that he did not disembark in Southampton until 18 June, sixteen days after Captain Tennant RN sent the signal 'BEF evacuated' and six days before the fall of Dunkirk on 24 June. What happened to John during this period is not known, but he and a number of his colleagues were reported missing, presumed captured or killed. Happily he and many others survived and somehow got back to England. In his case it was aboard a French fishing boat.

By 3 June and out of the jaws of near annihilation, four fifths of the BEF

68. John as Lieutenant Colonel with his son, David, and his father Frank in 1942.

69. John as Commanding Officer with the Bugle Platoon KSLI in 1942.

had been evacuated aboard an armada of assorted craft. Fortunately the weather held during those critical nine days. The poet John Masefield summarised this magnificent achievement:

The enemy had proclaimed our complete encirclement and destruction; no doubt he had expected to achieve both aims. He did not do these things because he could not. He came up against inundations and defences which checked his tanks; against soldiers who defied him and drove him back: against our Air Force which attacked him with complete indifference to the numbers he sent against it: against our Navy, which is a service apart. Lastly, he came up against the spirit of this Nation, which, when roused, will do great things.

Yet this brief and salutary experience must have left a lasting impression on all those fortunate enough to survive. Unless the British Army dramatically improved their manoeuvrability and fighting skills they would be no match for Hitler's Panzer Divisions.

The combination of Staff Training and his active service in France must have stood John in good stead for in July 1940 he was promoted Major and appointed General Staff Officer Grade 2 to 6th Corps in Ireland under the highly decorated and often wounded General Carton de Wiart VC, who wore a renowned black eye patch. Three months later John was appointed Instructor at the Senior Officers' School at Devizes and promoted Local Lieutenant Colonel, where he taught between October 1940 and July 1941. He was then appointed General Staff Officer Grade 1 for the North Wales Area as Acting Lieutenant Colonel while based in Shrewsbury for a year. To his delight in July 1942 he was appointed to command the 1st Battalion, The King's Shropshire Light Infantry, thus fulfilling his life's ambition.

Almost immediately the battalion moved to Callandar in Scotland and during the next seven months underwent rigorous training before sailing from Glagow to North Africa on 28 February 1943. It was during this period of training that John, drawing on his own experience of the North West Frontier and the lessons he had learned in France, did his utmost to ensure that his battalion was ready to fight the Germans and Italians in the desert and *jebel* terrain of North Africa. An extract from a letter to me dated 12 July 1999 from Lieutenant Colonel Dick Evans MC, who was a Support Platoon Commander at the time, is illuminating:

'It was not until your father arrived to take over command that we saw, felt and got a real impulse to prepare ourselves for active service. And any credit from this on the Battalion's ability in the North African Campaign was entirely due to his foresight, example and training. No wonder he got promoted at the end of it in May 1943.'

North African Campaign

Soon after docking at Bone on 11 March 1943, John was briefed that his Battalion was due to go into the line under command of the French almost immediately. By 2 April patrols north of Jebel–Bou–Arada towards Goubellat discovered that they were facing part of Hermann Goering's Panzer Division.

After extensive patrol activity the battle for Longstop Hill (Jebel-e-Ahmera) started early on Good Friday 23 April and raged through until the early hours of Easter Sunday 25 April, when the battalion was able to consolidate its position by holding a low range of hills overlooking the approaches to Tunis. As the area was heavily mined the assault had been from the flanks during which all companies came under heavy mortar and machine gun fire. Casualties during the assault on 24 April totalled 39 killed and 83 wounded. This was the battalion's first big attack and was regarded by higher authority as a first class achievement within six weeks of disembarking. It was for his action on 24 April that John was awarded the Distinguished Service Order, the citation for which is shown at Appendix 2.

Two days later on 27 April, battle resumed to the North for the horseshoe ridge of the Djebel-Bou-Aoukaz ('the Bou'), which dominated the Medjez-Tunis road and where the enemy and our own troops' position had been changing daily. This German counter attack, referred to as the 'Test Match', came close to breaking through but was finally repulsed. On 30 April John was promoted to command 3rd Infantry Brigade. Under command were 1st Battalion The Duke of Wellington's Regiment, 2nd Battalion The Sherwood Foresters and his own battalion.

Within days 3rd Infantry Brigade was briefly withdrawn in readiness to capture 'The Bou', which was believed to be the key to the battle and which, once permanently secured, would open the front door to Tunis. While 24th Guards Brigade had held it briefly and had won two Victoria Crosses in doing so, they had been viciously counter attacked and had been forced to withdraw.

Two extracts from *Personal Impressions of the Bou Aoukaz Action 5th and 6th May 1943* later written by Lieutenant Colonel Brian Webb-Carter, CO 1st Bn The Duke of Wellington's Regiment reflect well on John's contribution as Brigadier before and during this pivotal battle:

'I have attended a number of O groups, but never have I attended such a wildly improbable Brigadier's orders. Our cautious activity at the OP had been duly noticed, and the Bosche, resenting our presence and probably guessing its import, proceeded to knock hell out of the Grenadiers' positions. I thus got my first taste of what that devoted battalion had put up with until we had cleared the Bou. The Germans knew exactly where

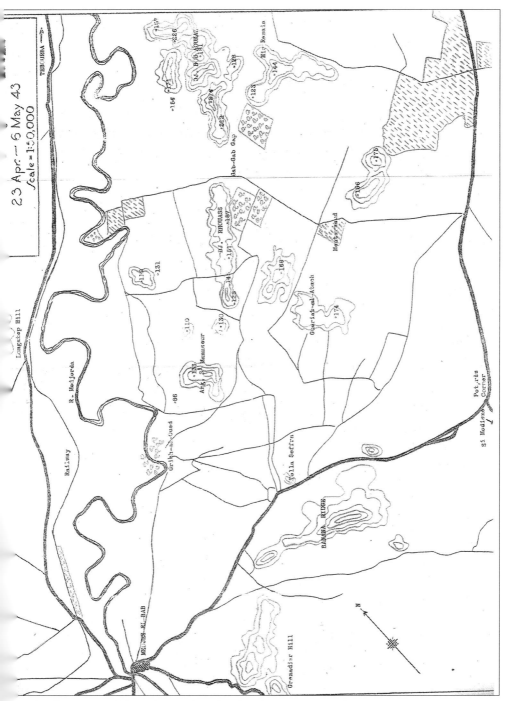

70. Sketch Map: The Advance from Medjez, Tunisia 23 April–6 May 1943.

Photograph courtesy of the Imperial War Museum, London

71. Soldiers of 1 KSLI beside a knocked out German tank in Tebourba; 8 May 1943.

the positions were and a hail of mortar and gun fire descended on Pt 171 and the feature behind it. With difficulty we made our way back to the Grenadiers' HQ and with the Brigadier in one slit trench, taking each CO in turn to give him his orders, the rest of us crouched in an adjacent trench. The whole position was systematically bombarded. My note book which I left on top of my trench was punctured – my pencil shattered.'

And later during the battle.

'Throughout that long night I felt enormously sustained by the clear cheerful note that could be discerned in all our Brigade Commander's directions. Harried as he must have been by the critical situation on the right, he gave us on the left every assistance, moral and material...'

On the 5 May, after air bombardment of the objective, an extended order assault by leading companies from the Duke's and the KSLI, supported by intense and accurate artillery fire, the Bou was finally secured on the 6 May. After a carefully preplanned heavy artillery barrage designed to give the enemy no time to regroup, the Allied main thrust by infantry and armour thundered towards Tunis. Cessation of hostilities in North Africa followed on 12 May 1943.

A fortnight later John wrote to Henry to congratulate him on becoming Commanding Officer of Auxiliary Patrol, Scapa Flow from HMS *Iron Duke*

72. John as Brigadier addressing some NCOs after cessation of hostilities in Tunisia.

in March. He also took the opportunity to relate his own recent experiences in North Africa.

P27213 Brig J G James
HQ 3rd Infantry Brigade
BNAF
May 26 1943
My Dear Hennie

> *So very many thanks for your letters – a delightful one before I left Scotland some months ago and another which I received out here.*
>
> *I do so congratulate you on your new command – it's a hell of a fine one and I only wish we were together so that we could suitably 'quench' the occasion! May our meeting come a good deal sooner than either of us expect. I arrived out in this part of the world at the beginning of March and now looking back on it all it seems a year ago since I was amongst civilisation – touching wood I've had the most amazing bits of luck (& I only trust that it lasts!) ever since I arrived out here.*
>
> *We were literally whizzed up from the port (our transport, mark you was still at sea, under your excellent care, making it's way slowly towards the port!) and we had to take over a portion of the front (I suppose I shouldn't mention names – yes, I will because it's all over now) down Bonarada Valley, from our friends the*

French! – we had to fight with borrowed stuff from other British Regiments.
I was in command of my battalion there for about a fortnight or so (one lost all
account of time) & actually things weren't half so bad as they were made out to
be by the previous occupiers! I had Senegalese on my right (NBG!) and Foreign
Legion (pretty good) on my left for part of the time, but the best that I saw were
our Tommies – a grand lot of men and didn't the Bosche like them, I don't think!
We were up against Mr Herman Bloody Goering's best division all the time –
the finest German troops they've got in most people's opinion – so my battalion
had to be on its mettle & by jove they were & I've never been prouder in my
life of any troops. One thing stuck in my mind & I've always insisted on in
training & that is Discipline & they had 100% and it carried them through
magnificently – we lost excellent chaps of course – we had a hell of a lot of
patrolling to do, but it was quite extraordinary how we gradually got the upper
hand of it – learning from the Bosche, who was a past master at the game, but
we always tried to go one better and did!
From that valley we were moved up to the Medjez-el-bab area & things really
got cracking as you know – the Battalion took part in various attacks – two
very major ones which had been costly failures to other units – & thanks to
God and guts they succeeded in both.
I was shortly put in command of the Brigade & wasn't I sorry to leave such a
Battalion, but thank goodness I still have them under my command in the
Brigade. Finally the Brigade had to attack an enormous mountain of a feature
called the Bou Aoukaz (the attack was referred to by Mr Atlee in his talk to the
house) which two other Brigades had failed to capture and hold. We made it &
as Mr Atlee so aptly said – General A's left was then firm! So that he could
manoeuvre with his right! – How simple it sounds! Now it's all over one is
relieved to the full & one feels rather like a bust balloon!
My luck consists of:
Whilst leaning against a carrier, it went up on a mine – carrier in bits, two of
the crew killed & the other two badly wounded – I was thrown about but
merely came down with a few pebbles (small ones) in my right knee – it was so
slight that I didn't get it dressed till that evening.
Three times lumps of shell have stuck into the bank within a few inches of
my head.
Whilst driving along in my jeep – preceding my Gunner officer – I looked
round to see him poor fellow go sky high on a mine with disastrous results.
Finally 4 days ago whilst flying & taking off from an aerodrome one hit a jeep
with the right wheel (damned fool in jeep was speeding down the runway!) as
we became airborne! I drew the pilot's attention to the large piece of iron (the
top strut of the wheel) which immediately had protruded through the right
wing and was slowly getting bigger. To cut a long story short we did a belly

flop (without wheels) on another aerodrome – magnificent piloting on the part
of the American – we were quite ok, but the plane written off. When we
eventually finished up in a field of daisies there were 5 ambulances (Yanks
call them Meat Boxes) awaiting us – we filled none!
We are now shortly going in on the next party – I have had to work with the
Senior Service a good deal of late – there is one Captain Robson (who knows
you well) also one Commander Archdale (I think that is his name – he knows
you) also a Rear Admiral – they're all a grand *lot.*
I must stop now & get down to work. I do so hope you are fit and well? When
you have a moment do drop me a line – God, if I could see England again.
We must thrash these swines first I suppose.
All the best always
Yours ever
John

Assault on the Island of Pantelleria 11 June 1943

The Island of Pantelleria lies midway between Tunisia and Sicily and stands
sentinel within the eighty mile strait separating the two. During June 1943 it
was a heavily fortified Axis outpost, viewed as a menace to the next stage in
the Allies' plans. Not only could it provide early warning of Allied deploy-
ment prior to assault landings on Sicily or Greece, but the 80 fighter planes
operating from Pantelleria's airfield could seriously harass any landing on
Sicily. Indeed the Allies needed this airfield to provide close air support for an
Assault Landing on Sicily as the airfields in North Africa were too far away.

This volcanic island's natural defences are formidable. It has higher and
steeper cliffs in the South East with ground rising, cut by lava streams, to
a central point some 2,700 ft above sea level. In the North West is a small
harbour with a town which at the time had about 4,000 inhabitants which
represented nearly half of the island's population.

Five years had been spent in strengthening the island's defences.
According to maps and aerial photographs at the time, fortifications of all
types from large coastal batteries to machine gun positions bristled all
around the coast and up in the hills behind. Concrete gun emplacements
and blockhouses had been sunk into the cliffs whilst tons of munitions were
stored in caves. According to intelligence reports there
was a garrison of 10,000 mainly Italian troops on the
island under command of Admiral Pavesi of the Italian
Navy. Mussolini boasted that 'Fortress Island' was
impregnable.

The British 1st Infantry Division was allotted the task
of taking Pantelleria. The 3rd Infantry Brigade, under

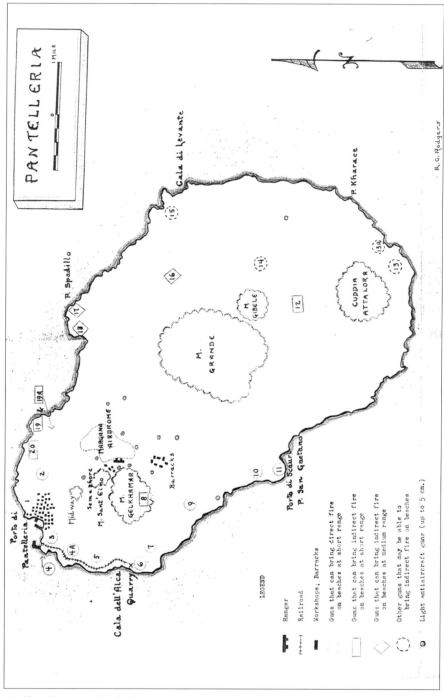

73. Sketch Map: Island of Pantelleria showing coastal defences.

John's command, was chosen to be the Assault Brigade on 'Operation Workshop'. After extensive aerial bombing and Royal Navy gunfire to soften up the island's defences the first two battalions, 1 DWR and 1 KSLI would land on Pantelleria on 11 June. Between 7 and 11 June in day and night air raids over 4,656 tons of bombs hit the island and over 57 enemy aeroplanes were shot down. The Royal Navy also wrought violent destruction on the coastal defences from the guns of five cruisers and eight destroyers. The cruiser HMS *Penelope* was hit by fire from the shore batteries but not seriously damaged.

The Assault Brigade embarked at Sousse on 10 June during an air raid and by 10 am next morning the force was lowered from parent ships into assault boats eight miles from the harbour at Pantelleria. It was a typical warm Mediterranean day with clear blue sky. Lieutenant Colonel Brian Webb-Carter, CO 1 DWR takes up the story.

'Seen from a distance, the island appeared to be one solid mountain mass rising straight out of the sea and that morning it looked grim and sinister enough. The lower slopes were shrouded in a huge grey dim coloured pall, which at first appeared to be morning mist, but which later we knew to be the clouds of dust and smoke left by our last bombing raid.'

'As we moved steadily nearer the shore, it was an impressive sight to look round and view the whole great convoy moving along in perfect formation with its escorts of cruisers and destroyers steaming ahead and to either flank. But the most impressive of all was when our bombers came over to blast the defences for the last time before we landed; that was a sight that none of us will forget.'

'Meanwhile we moved steadily nearer, and one could see flashes from the guns of our naval escort, as they too joined the bombardment. As each minute passed we expected to come under answering fire of the coastal batteries; they must – it seemed – be holding their fire to the last moment, and excitement grew more intense. Some of the destroyers were now within a few hundred yards of the shore, firing at point blank range, and still there came no reply from the guns on the island.'

The fierce naval and air bombardment continued until 11.30 am. The first assault craft reached the beach near the harbour at midday.

'Then, almost before we realised it, we were in the harbour, and already the leading troops were jumping out of the assault craft on to the moles. It seemed almost like some giant exercise and not real war as they scrambled over the great heaps of rubble that told of the colossal havoc wrought by our bombers, until one saw little groups of bewildered Italian soldiers hurrying to meet our troops with hands in the air.'

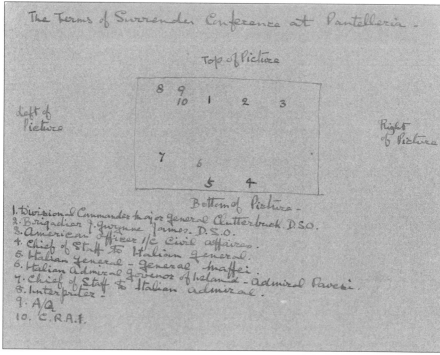

The Terms of Surrender Conference at Pantelleria.

Top of Picture

Left of
Picture

8 9
10 1 2 3

Right
of Picture

7
6

5 4

Bottom of Picture.

1. Divisional Commander Major General Clutterbuck. D.S.O.
2. Brigadier J. Gwynne James. D.S.O.
3. American officer I/c Civil affairs.
4. Chief of Staff to Italian General.
5. Italian General - General Maffei.
6. Italian Admiral Governor of Island - Admiral Pavesi.
7. Chief of Staff to Italian admiral.
8. Interpreter -
9. A/Q.
10. C.R.A.F.

Photograph courtesy of the Imperial War Museum, London

74. Opposite: Surrender Conference at Pantelleria on 11 June 1943. The reverse of this photograph bears the names of those present, in John's handwriting.

75. Above: Admiral Pavesi and his Chief of Staff. John is behind and to the left of the Admiral.

There was some small arms fire on the leading companies of 1 KSLI but it did not last and soon HMS *Laforey* reported seeing a white flag at the look-out station on Semaphore Hill.

'Suddenly a host of white flags appeared and everywhere little bands of soldiers, each armed with his own token of surrender, were making their way towards us, some preceded by a leader bearing a great white banner, almost as if at some Salvation Army rally.'

The leading companies went forward through the ruins to the first objective meeting no opposition.

'Throughout that day and the next, the prisoners poured in, soldiers, sailors and civilians – many of these last pathetic sights – all seemingly only too glad that their ordeal was over at last.'

By 5.30pm on 11 June it was all over when Admiral Pavesi signed the surrender document handing over his sword to Captain Hugh Ripley, 1 KSLI.[24] Mussolini's 'Fortress Island' had fallen.[25] The population of the island had been without food and water for three days. Less than 200 hundred defenders had been killed and about 200 had been wounded by the heavy bombing and naval gunfire. Own casualties were limited to those caused by German dive bombers after the surrender. 3rd Infantry Brigade had cleared the way to Sicily.

Assault Landing at Anzio on 22 January 1944

The Allied Invasion of Sicily followed one month later on 10 July 1943 and was by far the largest Assault Landing so far. This and the subsequent fighting to secure Sicily proved a massive experience from which to draw in planning for subsequent smaller assault landings at Salerno and Anzio, but most of all for the D Day landings in Normandy on 6 June 1944. As 3rd Infantry Brigade was not directly involved in Sicily or in Salerno, we shall pass by these crucial actions and move on to Anzio.

However, before doing so, the Allies' successful invasion of Sicily and their advance into mainland Italy in September, triggered some significant developments on the international scene. On 25 July the King of Italy dismissed Mussolini as Prime Minister and had him arrested. On 3 September 1943 Italy surrendered unconditionally leaving the Germans on their own to resist the Allies. To do so they would have to call for reinforcements from both Northern Europe and the Russian front. Churchill's strategic plan, which had many doubters among Chiefs of Staff in Washington, seemed to be working.

Nevertheless, following the costly failure of the opposed landing at Salerno, there followed a dismal deadlock during the fighting on mainland Italy, which was now in the grip of winter. The Germans had formed formidable defences on the Gustav Line, which ran from Cassino in the west to Ortona on the Adriatic. They were determined not to give ground. The Allies needed to keep up the pressure on the Germans to prevent troop transfers to France to repel the eagerly awaited invasion of North West Europe. The aim of the landing at Anzio, one of the boldest and most adventurous of Allied plans, was to cut into the rear of the German troops holding the Gustav Line and cause them to withdraw from Cassino.

However selecting Lieutenant General John P Lucas, GOC 6th Corps of the American 5th Army to command the operation was a strange choice because he was exhausted from the strain of the Salerno landing, where

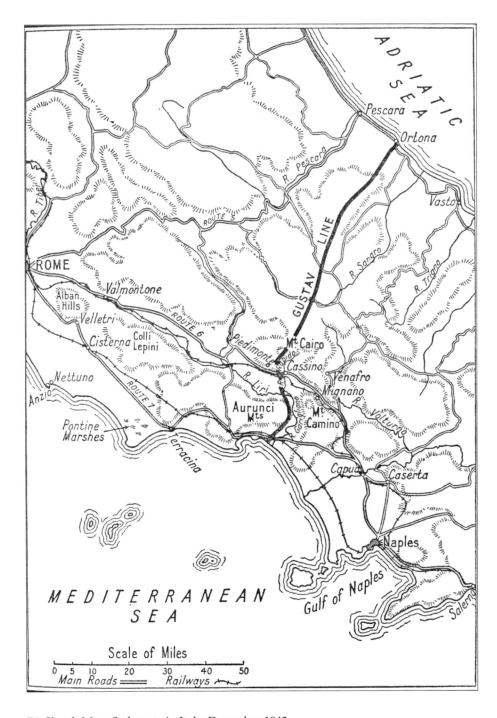

76. Sketch Map: Stalemate in Italy, December 1943.

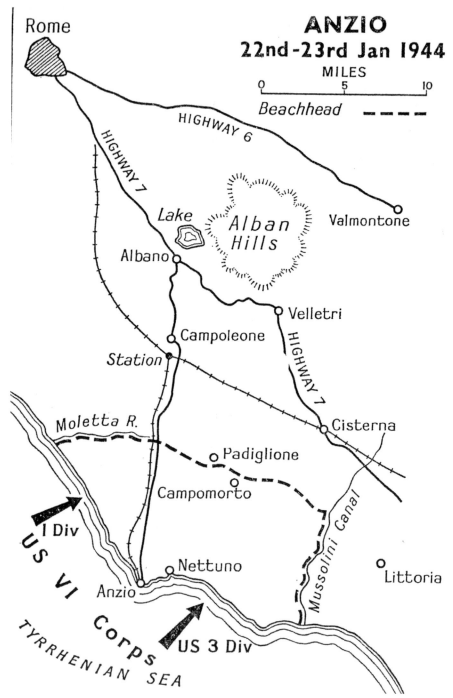

77. Sketch Map: The Landing at Anzio on 22 and 23 January 1944.

his unit had been mauled by a swift and violent counter attack commanded by Field Marshal Kesselring. As General Lucas left the final conference before the assault on Anzio, he was heard to mutter, 'This is going to be worse than Gallipoli!'

The troops under his command were the US 3rd Infantry Division under Major General Truscott, plus the 509 Parachute Infantry Battalion and the Rangers under Colonel Darby. Also under command was the 1st British Infantry Division commanded by Major General Penney. John was one of the three Brigade Commanders. While the British held a fairly successful rehearsal off the coast of Salerno, the American rehearsal was a disaster due to a navigational error, causing vehicles and men being unloaded into deep water and resulting in the loss of many men and much equipment.

In the days before the landing the main concern among the British Command was that General Lucas had decided he should first establish a bridgehead and then wait and see what happened. In response to General Penney's demand to know the exact plans, General Lucas sent a memorandum:

This directive does not include plans for an advance from the Beachhead to or towards the final objective. Such plans are extremely tentative. This advance will not take place unless it is synchronised with operations of the remainder of the 5th Army in close proximity to the Beachhead.

To the intense concern of the British Command there was no mention of any advance to the Alban Hills. All seemed geared to the defence of the Beachhead against vicious counter attack, much as had happened at Salerno. Not a good omen. News from the Cassino front was not encouraging. The First Allied attack on 17 January on the German 10th Army had got bogged down in the mud.

In 1944 Anzio was a small fishing port thirty miles south of Rome and sixty miles due west and behind Cassino. The area around Anzio was featureless and flat, interspersed with gullies and wadis. There was water a foot below the surface.

The invasion fleet of 253 ships carrying 35,000 men with tanks, guns and supplies were at anchor South of Anzio. The fleet had sailed during an air raid with Vesuvius lighting up the sky. By 7.30 am on 21 January they were off the beach. By midnight the Landing Ships Infantry (LSIs) were anchored in position for the assault landing craft, with their load of infantry, to swing out from the davits and to be lowered onto the sea. At 1am on 22 January the first assault wave headed for the shore. H Hour was 2am.

The assault was largely unopposed and the day went according to plan with 24th Guards Brigade and 2nd Infantry Brigade leading and moving north along the coast road. There were several encounters with small groups of German coastal defence units, but few casualties were sustained. 3rd Infantry Brigade under John was held in reserve. General Alexander stressed to General Lucas the importance of pushing on towards the Alban Hills and also sent a message to Churchill to this effect. Churchill's reply was 'Very glad you are pegging out claims, rather than digging in beachheads.'

However both Churchill and Alexander had been misled. No one was moving inland towards Cisterna or Albano. The force was occupying an area drawn in an 8 mile semi-circle around the port of Anzio. Lucas had been told by intelligence that Kesselring had the 29th and 90th Panzer Grenadier Divisions near Rome and so expected a counter attack at any moment. It later transpired that there were only two under strength divisions to defend Rome. The only formation near enough to engage the invading force was the weak 29th Panzer Grenadier Division which had been badly mauled and was unfit for action.

Consequently the road to Rome and the Alban Hills was wide open. Indeed it later transpired that on the eve of the Anzio Landing, Admiral Canaris, Chief of the German Counter-espionage, who was visiting Kesselring's headquarters at the time, had reassured everybody: 'There is not the slightest sign of a fresh landing; shipping in the port of Naples is quite normal.'

The Allies had achieved complete surprise. If they had been able to exploit it, how different the next few months could have been. The controversy about this decision still continues to this day.

When Kesselring received confirmation of the Allied Landing in the early hours of 22 January, he expected the Assault Force to reach Cisterna or Campoleone. Scarcely believing his luck that this had not happened, he wasted no time in dispatching all available German units to form a ring round Anzio. Every 88mm gun was sent to the area. By 23 January he had a mixed bag of eight divisions forming a defensive wall round the beachhead with another five divisions hastening to join them. Because the Allied attack on Cassino had failed, he recalled the 26th Panzer Division to Anzio. On the evening of 23 January the Luftwaffe attacked the Allied Beachhead. The road to Rome and the Alban Hills had been firmly shut.

The Campoleone Salient. 29 January–1 February 1944

Next morning cold winter rain coincided with the British 1st Division being released from reserve to probe towards Campoleone. News also came that 40,000 German troops were now in the vicinity of Anzio and that Hitler had ordered that no ground be given along the entire Gustav Line.

At dawn on 25 January, four days after the first landing, 24th Guards Brigade pushed forward up the Albano Road towards the Factory and houses at Carroceto. During the next twenty four hours, the ferocity and cost of the house-to-house fighting to secure it and repel the subsequent German counter attack were a salutory warning of the strength and resolve of the German cordon around the beachhead.

By 29 January, John's 3rd Brigade was deployed in the area of the Factory. General Penney, commanding British 1st Division, tasked 24th Guards Brigade to secure the start line – a lateral road – from which 3rd Brigade would launch their attack to capture the station at Campoleone, a further mile and a half up the railway line. However, a combination of events conspired to delay the securing of the start line. This critical delay forfeited any element of surprise and allowed Kesselring to redeploy more of his forces to Campoleone to resist the anticipated Allied attack. This railway line, part of the main line from Naples to Rome was raised on an embankment which was a severe obstacle to tanks and infantry. By now the Germans had deployed its tanks and machine guns to bring fire to bear on both the main road and embankment and had mined the bridge.

It was not until 3pm on 30 January that 1 KSLI on the right and 1 DWR on the left made their advance on the railway station. By nightfall 1 KSLI had secured a good ridge just short of the embankment, but 1 DWR had met strong opposition as they tried to get to the embankment in their sector.

While General Penney's Division had advanced twelve miles from the sea up the Anzio–Albano Road, the ground it now held had narrowed the further it had advanced. The leading Company Commander of 1 KSLI – at the extreme tip of the Division's advance declared: 'We feel like the lead in the pencil!' To make matters worse, the American 1st Armored, which were tasked to make a wide sweep on the left to carry them round Campoleone and on to the Alban Hills, had become bogged down in endless soft wadi beds and thirty feet deep dykes. Any immediate prospect of 3rd Brigade getting support from the Americans on their left help had evaporated.

The only alternative was to get the armour back to the main road and call upon the Sherwood Foresters in 3rd Brigade Reserve to make an all-out effort to capture Campoleone Station. The armour would then pass through and fan out onto the lower slopes of the Alban Hills.

After an artillery barrage, the gallant Sherwood Foresters advanced to be decimated in their tracks by well sighted German defences. By the end of a desperate day's fighting the Commanding Officer, Adjutant and all Company Commanders were casualties. No Company could muster more than forty all ranks and one company was down to twenty. That night the Battalion reported to 3rd Brigade HQ a fighting strength of only 8 Officers and 250 men. Any hope of an armoured breakthrough was abandoned. Later that night as 1st Armoured withdrew back along the Anzio-Albano

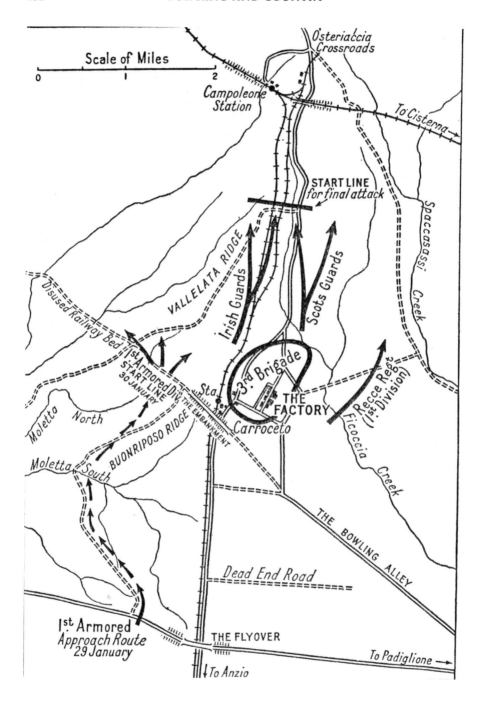

78. Sketch Map: The Advance to Campoleone, 29–30 January 1944.

Road and passed back through British 1st Division, not a man would have failed to realise what this meant to the Allied cause.

As for 3rd Brigade, more isolated than ever, it had been ordered to 'stay where you are and don't give an inch.' It was cramped in amongst the olive groves and vineyards just short of the fatal railway line. John's Brigade front did not extend more than two thousand yards and offered an inviting salient for German counter attacks on both flanks. On 3 February rain swept the beachhead neutralising any effective air cover.

On the world stage, the beachhead seemed one vast puddle with the Allies digging in to defend it. At this time Mr Churchill lamented '... I had hoped that we were hurling a wild cat on to the shore, but all we had got was a stranded whale.' In contrast, Hitler had followed the fortunes of his armies at both Cassino and Anzio with growing interest and excitement. Here at last was an opportunity to break the depressing sequence of German Army defeats since the end of 1942. German success here would bode well for their ability to smash the threatening Allied invasion of Northern France.

It was clear that any German counter attack would be made down the Anzio-Albano Road. However, General von Mackensen and his Fourteenth Army, who had acquired a healthy respect for the Allies fighting skills during the last few weeks, did not feel ready to strike a major blow just yet. Their three stage plan was a preliminary attempt to cut off 3rd Brigade, followed by an attack using stronger forces to capture the Factory area and Campoleone. From this start line they would then make an all out effort to smash through to the sea.

The layout of 3rd Brigade remained as before their final battle for Campoleone Station, although the badly mauled and now severely under strength Sherwood Foresters were now in reserve astride the Anzio-Albano Road. Unlike the remainder of British 1st Division which was over-dispersed behind them, 3rd Brigade was fairly compact. All companies were dug in and mutually supporting to cover the intervening gaps with mortar and machine gun fire and were waiting for the attack with confidence. The danger point lay behind them down the road towards Anzio, which seemed to invite enemy infiltration.

Withdrawal from the Salient. 2–4 February 1944

At eleven pm on 3 February the Germans, who had infiltrated between the wide gaps in the Guards Brigade west of the Anzio-Albano Road, launched a vicious attack on the Irish Guards. At dawn the Germans followed this with an attack from the east which swept in over on the 6th Gordons. In the chaos of battle the Irish fought magnificently and the Germans exploited a misunderstanding by the Scots, to tear a huge gap in the British position. By 10 am on 4 February

German tanks were sweeping the main road with fire. 3rd Brigade was cut off from the rest of the Division and in deadly peril. John, as Brigade Commander, was cut off from all three battalions under his command.

The driving rain neutralised any prospect of Allied Air support yet provided cover for the enemy to bring up reserves ready to reinforce their hold on the salient. Only accurate shooting from the beachhead artillery prevented these reserves being poured in as reinforcements. At this opportune moment General Penney, commanding British 1st Division, heard news of the arrival of British 168th Brigade at Anzio quayside. He pressed General Lucas to release this well tried Brigade from the Cassino front, to counter-attack. Barely twenty four hours ashore, the 1st London Scottish, chosen as fellow Scots to the Gordons, across whose ridge the attack would go in, moved north of the Factory to link up with the 46th Royal Tanks. H Hour for the counter-attack was 4 pm.

At this stage General Penney went forward to 3rd Brigade HQ, which was in a broken down farmhouse north of the Factory. Wynford Vaughan-Thomas, War Correspondent who was present at the time, describes the scene in his book *Anzio*.

> … but James was one of those steady men who can see a battle as a whole and estimate coolly the exact extent of the threatening danger. He sat in his jeep, while Penney waited in the command truck parked against the farmhouse wall. 'You'll have to get them out by daylight' he told James. 'Warn them to move'.
>
> James sent his orders by radio across the gap where the Germans waited to trap his men. All battalions were to get ready to break off contact with the enemy. The signal word for the move would be 'Tally Ho!' The DWR and the Foresters would move first, and the KSLI, at grips with the enemy on the right flank of the salient, would have the difficult task of forming the rearguard.

No one would envy General Penney or Brigadier James at this moment. Penney had done all he could to retrieve the situation by getting his hands on the only reinforcements available and swiftly tasking the 1st London Scottish to counter attack. If this failed, he stood to lose one third of his Division.

Equally John, now cut off from his Brigade, which included his own regiment, had to get the timing of the withdrawal just right or he stood to lose all those he had led since arriving in North Africa nearly a year earlier. All both men could do was keep each other company, pray and wait for news.

Soon after 4 pm came the good news that 1st London Scottish advance supported by tanks was going well. They had caught the Germans before they had consolidated their newly won ground and had managed to open

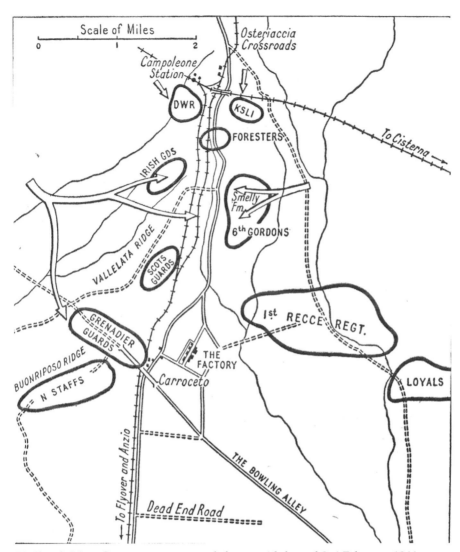

79. Sketch Map: German counter attack forces withdrawal 3–4 February 1944.

up a sort of corridor for 3rd Brigade to withdraw through. Next they heard that the Scots had run into heavy fire and had been forced to slow down short of their objective. As there was danger in delay James announced 'Tally Ho!' over the command net and the first stage of the planned withdrawal got under way.

As the Beachhead artillery put down concentrations of fire in a screen around the salient, weary rain drenched men stumbled their way in the dark back through 'the corridor' and on to the single road which soon became choked with marching columns, lorries and jeeps. The wounded were supported by their colleagues or hitched lifts on any nearby wheels. Small dispersed groups of Germans, lying huddled in broken buildings on each flank, opened up with machine guns on their retreating foes. German shells started to fall on the crowded roadway. To those like Wynford Vaughan-Thomas who watched,

> it seemed a chaotic drift towards dubious safety, a mob of defeated men driven before the Germans.

> Appearances were deceptive. There were dead everywhere, with tanks and smoke rolling over the shell-torn fields. Very lights soared and tracers flashed in all directions. Yet when the last units got in after mid-night and the roll-calls were taken, with the men standing drugged with fatigue half-asleep in their muddy ranks, 3rd Brigade had cause to be proud of itself. The battalions had to leave sorely needed equipment behind; tanks and anti-tank guns were abandoned and lorries left to burn, but the Brigade was still intact as a fighting unit (the KSLI had even knocked out two tiger tanks). This was the reward that had been torn from the jaws of almost certain death.

The Germans had failed to cut off 3rd Brigade, which had withdrawn two and a half miles back down the road towards Anzio. Yet Hitler had tasted blood and intelligence reports soon confirmed a steady build up of more and more German units from Northern Italy, the South of France and the Balkans. A stronger German attack could be expected at any time.

Defence of Carroceto. 7–10 February 1944

General Penney needed to redeploy his available forces to defend Carroceto village as soon as possible. 3rd Brigade and the Irish Guards who had borne the brunt of the recent fighting in the salient were to be placed in reserve. It was on 11 February that General Lucas wrote a letter to General Penney to congratulate him on the magnificent contribution of British 1st Division. A copy of this letter, over-marked by John, is shown at Appendix 3.

However there was to be no respite for anyone because between 7 and 20 February the Germans attacked the beachhead with ten divisions against the Allied five. For a week the two armies fought each other to exhaustion and stalemate. It was not until 20 February that the crisis was over and the Allied line restabilised.

The Allies had fought an extremely successful and gallant defensive battle and had resisted all stages of the German plan to drive them back into the sea. However, it had clearly failed to cut off the German XIVth Army behind Cassino. It was to be a further three months of unrelenting defensive warfare before the Allies were ready to break out of the beachhead in May.

Although John continued to command 3rd Brigade for much of this time, defensive tactics do not catch the eye like his pivotal role in the salient had done earlier. This fact and the imminent arrival of his successor during March and his transfer in April to command 36th Infantry Brigade at Cassino, renders it more difficult to chronicle his contribution during his remaining weeks in Anzio Beachhead.

Anzio with hindsight

Because the Anzio landing, which had achieved complete surprise but had failed to cut off the German XIVth Army and force its withdrawal from the Cassino front, it has often been portrayed as an expensive failure. Indeed the appointment of General Truscott to replace General Lucas as Allied Force Commander on 17 February, seemed to make Lucas the scapegoat for Allied frustration at his perceived lack of opportunism and aggression. However, with the benefit of hindsight, this all needs to put in context. Interestingly three Allied Generals agree that early opportunism would have been disastrous: General (later Field Marshal) Sir Gerald Templer, then a Divisional Commander at Anzio, told Nigel Nicholson, author of *Alex*:

'I never understood how Anzio could possibly work. I am absolutely convinced that if Lucas had gone on (which he could have) he could have got to Rome, but within a week or fortnight there wouldn't have been a single British soldier left in the bridgehead. They would all have been killed or wounded or prisoners. We would have had a line-of-communications forty five miles long from Anzio to Rome with absolutely open flanks. The Germans produced seven divisions in ten days, with plenty of armour, and we wouldn't have had a chance.'

General Mark Clark also commented to Nigel Nicholson in 1970:

'We had a small and inadequate landing force. After experiencing difficulties at Salerno, I had requested that we land with three divisions. We landed with two – one British and one American, and the British Division was not full strength. It was not possible that upon landing we could just move in and occupy the Alban Hills. The German reaction to our landing was swift. We had broken the German code and could read the messages from Hitler to 'drive us into the sea and drown us.' He also ordered several divisions from France, Germany, Yugoslavia and from other sectors of Italy to the bridgehead. Knowing of the impending onslaught, it was necessary to dig in, for had we advanced, we would have surely been defeated. Alex and I discussed these problems and decided to dig in and reinforce as rapidly as possible.'

Field Marshal Lord Carver, who served in Italy in 1943 as a twenty-eight year old Lieutenant-Colonel in command of the 1st Royal Tank Regiment, wrote in his book, *War in Italy 1943-1945:*

'The unfortunate Lucas was undoubtedly right not to have tried to thrust rapidly inland from Anzio before he had secured a firm and large enough beachhead. To have done so would almost certainly have led to disaster. Only a major amphibious assault, on the scale at least of Salerno, would have produced better results, and it would need to have been accompanied by a stronger attack against the Gustav Line than that made in January.'

General Sir Gerald Templer concluded that Lucas had been right by accident: 'I don't think he took the decision at all. I think he just failed to do anything else. He was absolutely full of inertia, and couldn't make up his mind. He had no qualities of any sort as a commander, absolutely no presence: he was the antithesis of everything that a fighting soldier and general should be.'

In short and with the benefit of hindsight, Lucas had become a perfect scapegoat for those whose expectations of Anzio had been unrealistically high.

Transfer to 36th Infantry Brigade at Cassino. April 1944

As a schoolboy I had often wondered why my father, John, had been transferred from commanding 3rd Infantry Brigade at Anzio to command 36th Infantry Brigade at Cassino in March/April 1944. It seemed a strange thing to happen at the height of both battles. It was not until I myself was Adjutant of the KSLI depot in Shrewsbury in 1961 that I discovered why this had happened.

Colonel 'Bunny' Careless, who had commanded 1 KSLI at Anzio, came bustling in to my office clutching a recently published book, entitled 'Desert Generals' by Corelli Barnett, the military historian. He was clearly spitting nails about what he had just read in the book, slammed it down on my desk and said 'I'll tell you what really happened!'

It all centred on a certain Major General E. Dorman-Smith, whom Colonel 'Bunny' considered had played a significant part in ghostwriting certain sections of Corelli Barnett's book. Two appendices totalling eleven pages and frequent reference to him in the index seemed to support this theory.

Major-General Dorman-Smith, who was a brilliant Staff Officer, became Deputy Chief of Staff to General Auchinleck, Commander-in-Chief the Near East on 16 June 1942. Between 25 June and 4 August the same year he acted as General Auchinleck's Operations Officer at Headquarters Eighth Army in

North Africa. When General Alexander replaced General Auchinleck on 6 August 1942, Major-General Dorman-Smith was also relieved as Deputy CGS, reduced to the rank of Brigadier and returned to England. Soon after his dismissal by Prime Minister Churchill, he sued Churchill for the phrase in his book, '… and restore confidence in the command, which I regret does not exist at the present time.' The case was settled out of court, Churchill agreeing to insert a long footnote in future editions of his *Memoirs*. Amongst other things this footnote absolves Dorman-Smith from any responsibility for the fall of Tobruk or the defeats at Gazala. It also refers to Rommel's remarkable tribute about the handling of the Eighth Army at the time.

Nevertheless Dorman-Smith's reputation for being a theorist unfit for direct command, was preventing him from being granted a field command, despite his many requests to be given such an opportunity. Ultimately and according to Colonel 'Bunny' Careless, Dorman-Smith wrote to Churchill who finally succumbed to pressure and agreed to speak to General Alexander requesting that Dorman-Smith be appointed to command one of the best Brigades under his command. He in turn spoke to General Penney, commanding British 1st Division at Anzio, who with considerable reluctance chose 3rd Brigade. John handed over his Brigade to Brigadier Dorman-Smith during March 1944, moved to the Cassino front and took over command 36th Infantry Brigade in April. Two months later he was killed.

According to Appendix C in Corelli Barnett's book, Dorman-Smith 'delivered a model attack on the Aquabona ridge after which the division was in reserve until August 1944. However, in August 1944, as the Brigade moved into the front at Florence, Dorman-Smith was *suddenly and unexpectedly removed from its command by the Divisional Commander on the grounds that he was unfit for Brigade Command.'*

Colonel 'Bunny' Careless explained why. He said that John had commanded 3rd Brigade by getting forward to read the battle and the Battalion Commanders and his Brigade Staff respected his abilities as a leader of the finest Brigade that any of them had served in. In contrast Dorman-Smith preferred to stay well back, was rarely seen and was full of theories and was considered a poor field commander.

Colonel 'Bunny'also told me of a particular incident which shows the rising tensions between Commanding Officers and their new Brigade Commander at the time. When news arrived in 3rd Infantry Brigade on 26 June that John had been killed while commanding 36th Infantry Brigade near Lake Trasimene, his former Brigade and his many friends in his regiment were all much saddened by his loss. As CO, Colonel 'Bunny', who had served with John for many years, wanted to discover what had happened and to represent the KSLI at his funeral to ensure that John's ultimate resting place would be fitting. By then both Brigades were deployed north of Rome and it was a relatively simple matter of a drive of no great distance from one Brigade area to another. As the KSLI were in reserve at the time, he asked Brigadier Dorman-Smith for a short leave of absence. When this was refused, he was naturally incensed and after giving careful instructions to his Second-in-Command to take over command, he drove off to represent 3rd Brigade and the KSLI at John's brief funeral in the field. On his return to the KSLI area later in the day, he was called for by his Brigadier and severely admonished for being absent without leave. This episode merely increased existing tensions still further.

After six months of acute frustration at their new Brigade Commander's lack of field command skills, the three battalion commanders formed up to General Penney in August 1944 simply saying 'Either he goes or we do.' Penney had no choice. This incident just reinforces the fact that brilliant staff officers seldom make the best field commanders. Perhaps I can be forgiven for wishing that all this had never happened.

Cassino to Rome. April to 4 June 1944

It must have been hard for John to leave 3rd Brigade in April 1944 to make way for Brigadier Dorman-Smith. He was leaving an outstanding brigade which included his own regiment and many friends who had fought with him for a year, since arriving in North Africa in March 1943. However, there were some consolations. He was being appointed to command 36th Infantry Brigade, part of 78th Division on the Cassino front. This Division, whose soldiers wore the Battle-Axe divisional flash with pride, had an exceptional fighting record in North Africa, Sicily and Italy. Since being formed in June 1942, it had cultivated an unusual understanding between staff and the fighting units. Although little known to the general public, it was much respected by the rest of the British Army and enjoyed a tremendous ésprit de corps. John was taking over command of his Brigade at a critical stage in the battle for Monte Cassino.

Already three major battles had failed to dislodge the Germans from this dominating feature. The Allied advance had now been stopped in its tracks since January. Under his command were now the 5th Buffs, 6th Royal West Kents and the 8th Argyll and Sutherland Highlanders; his new Divisional Commander was Major General Charles F Keightley CB DSO OBE.

No records show the date in April that John arrived to take over command of 36th Infantry Brigade from Brigadier Spencer. However, at the end of April the whole Division was withdrawn to rest in the green valley of Capua thirty miles away, where the guns were out of earshot. This was the

Division's first real respite since it had landed in North Africa eighteen months earlier. This was badly needed because its morale had been bruised by a series of hard and furious battles and heavy casualties.

'Its two months in the Cassino battlefield had been perhaps the dreariest and unhappiest in its history, for the losses and hardships it had suffered had been – it seemed – to no purpose.' *History of the 78th Division.*

While John could be forgiven for feeling that he too deserved a rest after three months in the Anzio beachhead, this also gave him the opportunity to get to know those who he was shortly to lead in the fourth and final battle for Monte Cassino.

Every man had six days leave at rest camps at either Maiori or other places on the Sorrento peninsula. Day trips for the more enterprising included visits to Capri, Pompeii and Naples. General Keightley's belief was that there was no better morale-builder than the most intensive training. John did not need converting and it also gave him the opportunity to lead his new brigade for the first time. On 1 May this training began in earnest with river crossings exercises, street fighting and infantry tank cooperation.

During the three months that the Germans had denied the Monastery to the Allies, air photographs showed that the Germans had constructed defences along the far bank of the Rapido, which ran at right angles across Highway 6 and the entrance to the Liri Valley.

Alexander's new plan was an attack between the Monastery and the sea along a front of about nineteen miles. On the right, the Polish Corps was to attack the Monastery from the North West and then swing across Highway 6, the road to Rome, north of Cassino. In the centre, 4th British and 8th Indian Divisions were to force a crossing of the Rapido. On the left the French and US Corps were to strike north-west capturing Mounts Maio and Ausonia. At an appropriate moment in the battle the British and American Divisions were to break out from the Anzio beachhead and cut off the German's retreat. The role of the 78th Division was that of follow through reserve with an Armoured Brigade under command. The fourth battle for Cassino started at midnight on 11 May.

On the 14 May, 78th Division, after two weeks respite, were called forward to follow through the crossing of the Rapido where the bridge-heads varied between 500 and 1500 yards and to advance to the line of the Cassino-Pignataro road. At this stage in the battle 36th Infantry Brigade remained in reserve. During the next four days the Division fought with outstanding gallantry as is recorded in *Algiers to Austria, A History of the 78th Division during the Second World War* by Cyril Ray. Their *'cutting of Highway 6 turned the Monastery from a fort into a death trap for its occupants, and on 18th May the red and white flag of Poland could be seen flying from the grey ruins.'* Monte Cassino had finally fallen.

As darkness fell on the same day 36th Infantry Brigade took over the lead. The Argylls and Buffs moved forward towards the aerodrome just short of the town of Aquino. On their left the flash of guns showed that the Derbyshire Yeomanry were engaging the occupied houses at the forward edge of the town.

However, as it turned out an over-optimistic message from the Derbyshire Yeomanry that night, reporting that they were in Aquino, was the basis for next day's plan of attack. This was for the Brigade to occupy the town, covered by the fire of three field regiments of Royal Artillery and supported by Canadian tanks. This would trigger the Derbyshire Yeomanry and the Rifle Brigade to swing round the town and through the Adolf Hitler Line.

But air photographs did not show that there was a deep ravine, almost impassable to tanks, beyond and to either side of the town. The tanks were severely delayed. Next the Argylls and Buffs were checked just short of the town by previously unseen wire, and were raked by fire from concrete emplacements beyond. Both battalions were pinned down for a long hot day before being withdrawn under cover of 11 Infantry Brigade. Each battalion suffered thirty casualties, which included the CO of the Argylls, Lieutenant-Colonel Taylor MC who was wounded and the CO of the Buffs, Lieutenant-Colonel Monk MC, who was killed.

However, despite this gamble failing to come off, the Adolf Hitler Line was soon to crack. This line, which was not as strong as the Gustav line, ran across the Liri Valley for several miles in more open country. On 20 May General Keightley wrote to 36th Infantry Brigade to congratulate them on their long approach march and subsequent attack to break through the Adolf Hitler line during the preceding days. A copy of his letter, which is over-marked by John 'My Brigade!' at the top, is shown at Appendix 4.

While it had made military sense to try to rush the Adolf Hitler Line to disrupt the retreating Germans before they could re-establish themselves in their new prepared defences, these early attacks did not carry enough weight to break through. On 23 May the Eighth Army launched a set piece attack to smash through the Adolf Hitler Line. At the same time General Truscott launched the Anzio Force to finally break out from the beachhead and drive to cut off the Germans retreating from the main front. General Alexander's Allied plan and timing deceived Kesselring and achieved complete surprise.

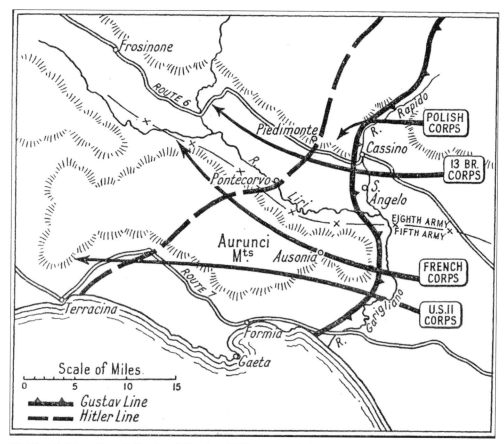

80. Sketch Map: Fourth Battle of Cassino. Fifth and Eighth Armies break through.

On the 24 May the 1st Canadian Division breached the Adolf Hitler Line. Next day the Poles completed its destruction by taking Piedimonte. On the same day General Truscott's Anzio force captured Cisterna and linked up with the rest of the Fifth Army who were advancing up the coast. Both German Armies – the Tenth and the Fourteenth – were in poor shape. The Tenth was now in full retreat from the main front and the Fourteenth was being badly mauled east of Anzio. By 25 May Truscott's spearheads had nearly reached Valmontone and next day would be astride the main German line of withdrawal. The trap was closing.

General Clark's obsession for being first into Rome

Then came an astonishing change of plan. On 25 May General Truscott received orders from General Clark to redirect his main thrust to the north-west and to head straight for Rome.

General Truscott has described how he felt,

'I was dumbfounded... This was no time to drive north-west where the enemy was still strong; we should pour our maximum power into the Valmontone Gap to ensure the destruction of the retreating German Army. I would not comply with the order without first talking to General Clark in person. Brann (his G3 Staff Officer) informed me that he was not in the beachhead and could not be reached even by radio... such was the order that turned the main effort of the beachhead forces from the Valmontone Gap and prevented the destruction of the German Tenth Army. On the 26th the order was put into effect.'

A meeting between the two generals three weeks earlier had prompted Truscott to note in his memoirs that Clark 'was fearful that the British were laying devious plans to be the first into Rome.' While Clark himself has written, 'On the other hand, as I have pointed out, I was determined that the Fifth Army was going to capture Rome, and I was probably oversensitive to indications that practically everybody else was trying to get into the act.'

Clark's obsession for being first into Rome was curious because there was never any question of anybody other than the Fifth Army capturing Rome. General Alexander had clearly laid down the inter-army boundary before the battle began. As the battle progressed it was constantly impressed on the Eighth Army that they had no immediate concern with Rome; their job was to draw the German Tenth Army into battle and destroy as much of it as possible. When the time came, they would by-pass Rome and continue the pursuit northwards. In General Truscott's recorded afterthoughts on the campaign he wrote:

There has never been any doubt in my mind that had General Clark held loyally to General Alexander's instructions, had he not changed the direction of my attack to the north-west on 26th May, the strategic objective of Anzio would have been accomplished in full. To be first in Rome was poor compensation for this lost opportunity.

Clark's fixation that British forces were plotting secretly to trespass on Fifth Army territory must have been a figment of his romantic and harassed imagination. His decision to make this fatal change of direction must remain one of the mysteries of the Italian Campaign. Through it the Allies had lost an outstanding opportunity to inflict a comprehensive defeat on the German Tenth Army, who had now been offered a life line. Kesselring's skilful and stubborn men exploited this to the full to fight again with increasing ferocity at Hannibal's battlefield near Lake Trasimene.

Back to 36th Infantry Brigade, 78th Division

Within a few days 36th Infantry Brigade, who were on the left of the 38th
Irish Brigade, were pushing steadily forward up Highway 6 towards
Frosinone, en route for Rome. But at this stage the German withdrawal
became particularly skilful as they slipped from one good position to
another at night, leaving roads, verges, villages and bridge-approaches
mined and booby-trapped. Snipers and mortar fire continually imposed
further delay. However, a combination of determination, guts and a growing skill and familiarity with the deadly obstacles left behind, ensured that
the enemy were pressed hard and given no respite.

Soon the Argylls were leading, supported by a troop of Wiltshire
Yeomanry and a pioneer platoon to clear the mines. Because all bridges on
Highway 6 had been blown, diversions had to be found and the mines lifted.
As tanks got bogged down, infantrymen helped their crews to shove and
heave at them over streams and gulleys and through thickly planted
orchards and olive groves. This was a slow and painstaking process always
at the mercy of snipers and mortar fire. In one morning the Argylls lost two
men killed and twelve wounded.

Meanwhile the Royal West Kents, who were working through rough
country to the north, met stiff opposition from rearguards supported by
self-propelled guns. When the Buffs took over the lead on 30 May, their
supporting tanks had difficulty in keeping up with the infantry. Near Ripi
they encountered opposition from rearguard troops and six tanks were dealt
with by our guns. Enemy artillery fire was at times intense and the Buffs
suffered casualties including one company commander wounded, but a
night patrol reported that Ripi was clear. The 38th Irish Brigade was ordered
to take San Giovanni and to link up with John's Brigade. The town was
strongly held and after two hours fierce street fighting by the London Irish
and the 3rd Hussars, it was taken.

The whole German front was in full retreat. By 1 June the Fifth Army,
who had linked up with the Anzio forces were about twenty miles from
Rome. They had broken through to cut Highway 6 east of Valmontone, so
making it impossible for the Germans to counter attack on the southern
front with any hope of success.

On the 78th Division front the Germans were now falling back with little
serious attempt to delay the advance except for demolitions and mortaring.
The Canadians had taken Frosinone on Highway 6 on 31 May and the
Indians were in the process of taking Veroli on the right flank. This enabled
the Argylls to be carried forward in trucks and unload west of Frosinone on
1 June with orders to clear the road to Alatri six miles north and then to
capture the town. Scout cars of 56th Recce Regiment skirmished up the

road while 'A' Squadron of the Wiltshire Yeomanry was to give support to the Argylls.

The following extract is from *Algiers to Austria, A History of 78th Division during the Second World War* by Cyril Ray.

'At first light on 2nd June the Argylls advanced and had soon captured Monte San Angelo and Monte Caprara on either side of the road. Soon they were a mile short of Alatri, a small town atop an olive clad hill. From here the Germans could command the approaching road and the bridge at the foot of the hill. The well preserved ancient walls were thirty feet high in places.'

As a direct assault was impossible, Lieutenant Colonel Taylor decided to surround the town. 'B' Company was ordered to move west on to Monte San Francisco and 'Y' Company to take the Monastery on the hill to the north of the town. It was a hot day and the hills were steep and rocky, the valleys deep. The tanks had not yet arrived so the company, commanded by Captain Davies, advanced without them. A platoon was sent up to the monastery walls from where an assault could be made. They climbed 300 feet up the steep hill and half way up came under machine-gun fire which they were soon able to silence, and they reached the top to find a solid stone wall eight feet high, its gate the only entrance to the monastery. In the absence of tanks, a hole was blown in the wall with a Piat, large enough for Lieutenant Stephen and his patrol to crawl through. They found the monastery unoccupied, the town in full view, and the enemy's way of escape to the north within easy machine-gun range.

The enemy were directing accurate shell-fire on the road to the south but the tanks below secured sixteen direct hits on the clock-tower, which the enemy was using as his observation post. At 4pm two companies of the Royal West Kents attacked the town, and the Germans robbed the watching Argylls of the cream of victory by slipping away down the road to the west – the one road which was not overlooked by the monastery.'

By now 78th Division had marched and fought thirty miles across broken country in five days. As they were given a well deserved rest in Corps reserve, General Keightley passed on to all units a letter of congratulations he had received from the Army Commander, General Leese on 7 June. A copy of this is shown at Appx 5.

Meanwhile the Americans of the Fifth Army, at the centre of the advance, were now only eight miles from Rome. Shortly after dawn on Sunday 4 June 1944, Rome fell as American tanks entered the city suburbs to the ringing of church bells and bombardments of flowers. The Germans had withdrawn to the north and had left it open. The battle now swept beyond Rome as the two armoured divisions who were leading the Eighth Army's advance were lifted to a concentration area at Rignano fifteen miles north.

In twenty four days the forces of Alexander had advanced eighty miles, broken through three defensive lines and had shattered the German Tenth Army. Rome was ours at last, but the triumph had been so long delayed, and the cost so heavy – at Anzio, Cassino and the Liri valley – that as 78th Division rested for just under a week at Alatri, it could only think of Rome as a leave town for a happier future.

Two days later the Allied Armies landed in France.

Rome to Lake Trasimene. 4 to 26 June 1944

On 8 June the division were called forward north of the city, to the west of the Tiber and heading towards Orvieto. As they moved forward to their new area, they will have seen two vivid and contrasting sights. Firstly, the roads littered with the debris of a retreating army – burnt out vehicles and tanks and broken equipment – stark evidence of allied air attack and long-range artillery bombardment. Secondly, a distant and tantalising glimpse of Rome.

During the last week or so, some of the division had the opportunity of visiting Rome. Extracts from John's letter to Anne dated 12 June show that he had remembered it was my seventh birthday and that he had been one of the fortunate few to visit Rome.

Letter 99
P27213 Brig J G James DSO
HQ 36 Inf Bde
June 12 1944
My own Darling

Today 7 years ago I remember so well my darling, you dear darling thing how can I ever thank you for giving me such happiness always. It is a <u>shame</u> that I can't be with you today – wouldn't it be fun? & I can picture you all so well in that sweet house of ours – oh how I long to be amongst you again! …

I went into Rome two evenings ago with one of the COs – we had a quiet dinner – could only stay for two hours and then came out again. What I saw of the city was indeed beautiful. Now I am well north of it plodding along! Sometime I trust I shall be able to see Rome properly – also the troops so richly deserve the honour.

I ran into Webb-Carter (CO 1 DWR). His battalion is on police duty in Rome! – lucky devils – my Brigade and Division is always busily engaged with the Bosche! But each day brings me nearer coming home, my darling – & the time is certainly going quickly. The Bosche is certainly going back pretty fast!!!

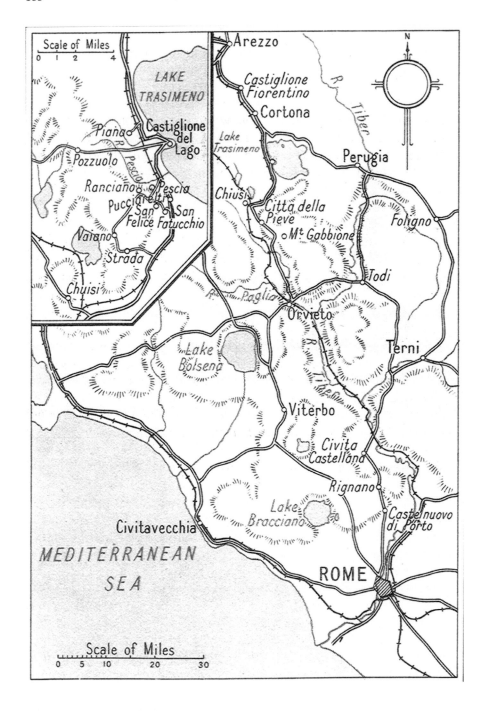

81. Sketch Map: Rome to Lake Trasimene.

I feel the war must end a good bit sooner than later now.
God Bless you, my darling & I love you so, you know that.
John
xxxxxx

The rate of advance towards Orvieto was governed by congestion on the roads caused by cluttered wreckage and sporadic German resistance. Most of the time the division was entering towns and villages already taken by the Americans or South Africans and were being greeted by cheering Italians bearing flowers and wine.

Orvieto declared an open city

At about this stage Major Richard Heseltine, commanding A Squadron of 3rd Hussars, who were pressing forward across the Viterbo plain towards Orvieto, witnessed a remarkable incident, which he describes in his book, *Pippin's Progress, A Soldier Artist's War.* His squadron was in the lead when Orvieto, perched on top of a high rocky outcrop, first came into view in the distance. Suddenly his leading Troop Commander reported that a German VW displaying a white flag was approaching. Perhaps it was surrendering?

Richard told his Troop Commander to intercept and escort the car back to him. In the car was a driver and an Oberleutnant who spoke perfect English, who handed over a written message. The opening sentence was: *In consideration of the historic beauty of Orvieto the German Command proposes to the Allied Command that they jointly declare Orvieto as an open city.* There followed various undertakings required from both sides, which were to be met in good faith.

Richard halted his Squadron and contacted his CO, Lieutenant-Colonel Sir Peter Farquhar, DSO and Bar, OBE (known as 'Colonel Push On') on the command net. Richard then dispatched the German Envoy under escort to RHQ. The CO then passed the Envoy to Brigade where a pact was finally agreed. Three hours after being first sighted, the VW sped back through A Squadron and headed back towards Orvieto.

Although not unique – for Assissi was to be declared open not long afterwards – it was a pause in hostilities and restored some confidence in human nature. Much later A Squadron halted close to the city's steep entrance. Richard said to his driver, 'Let's go and have a look!'

'So we climbed into my jeep and the two of us drove up the steep incline and through the gateway into the narrow thoroughfares. As our jeep clattered through the empty streets, it seemed a dead city. Everyone was in hiding. Fearing they would suffer the same fate as the citizens of Viterbo, they had descended into their many cellars hewn out of the tufa rock. Suddenly we debouched into the piazza and stopped, transfixed by the splendour of the cathedral's glistening façade, surely one of the most sublime sights in Italy. As Geoff and I sat there in amazement and wonder, someone noticed our uniform and then the whole town came running and engulfing us in joy. Thus were we the liberators of Orvieto, and this beautiful and historic city remained untouched. But the full credit is entirely due to the German general who initiated the whole project. I have often wondered if he ever returned in happier times, or perhaps he did not survive the war – who knows?'

Kesselring's Albert Line south of Lake Trasimene

With Orvieto behind and after crossing the River Paglia and half way to Lake Trasimene, it was at midday on 15 June that the Germans put up some stiff resistance at Monte Gabbione. While this was overcome by the Northamptons, further resistance at Citta della Pieve managed to repel the East Surreys.

An extract from John's penultimate letter to Anne dated 16 June shows how much he was longing for a rest and for the end of the war.

Letter 100 P27213 Brig J G James DSO
June 16 1944 HQ 36 Inf Bde
My dear Darling
   … Yes I am glad you are so delighted at the news out here – it's certainly <u>good</u>.
   My Bde is plodding along & one longs for a <u>rest</u> – but let us pray that the
   infernal war must end sometime fairly soon.
   I am looking forward to hearing all about David's birthday party!! Must stop
   now darling – I'm very fit & well. Hold thumbs for me always.
   All my love, beautiful
   Ever your own
   John
   xxxxxx

36th Infantry Brigade was sent forward to by-pass the town. After meeting opposition from snipers and machine guns, by dark on 18 June it was well north. For the first 500 yards they advanced along the crest of a ridge in full view of Citta della Pieve, before turning on to the main road through thick woods surrounding the town.

That evening an enemy wireless message was intercepted giving the time of the enemy withdrawal. At precisely that time plus five minutes the whole divisional artillery plastered the exits from the town for two minutes. As the Buffs took over from the East Surreys the next morning, the outskirts of the town were littered with bodies of German paratroopers. The few who remained subjected both the Buffs and the Royal West Kents to some of the deadliest sniping so far. But the enemy's final position was overcome by both battalions, who pushed through the town to the high ground beyond.

Battle for Cimbano Villastrada and Vaiano 19 – 22 June 1944

According to *The Trasimene Line June – July 1944* by Janet Kinrade Dethick, John was temporarily commanding 78th Division at this stage, probably to allow the Divisional Commander a brief respite. This was John's first experience of commanding the Division and a taster before his anticipated promotion to Major General.

Since the Cassino breakout the Allies had pressed forward relentlessly to prevent the Germans from establishing another defensive line. Now they were approaching the place where Hannibal had destroyed a Roman Army in his march from the north towards Rome.[26] What was now in store for Alexander's forces? Mindful of this ancient history and recognising the defensive potential of such a battleground, the Allies pressed forward with ever increasing urgency.

An extract from *The Trasimene Line* reports:

Brigadier James, commanding 78th Division, sent 36th Brigade into the attack at Villastrada on 20th June. Although the village was liberated, the Germans repulsed the follow-through attack, which he then launched on Vaiano.

Just at this time the rain came to hamper the advance and stifle air support. This gave the enemy the opportunity to strengthen his defences. The Argylls, leading 36th Infantry Brigade towards Vaiano over rugged country, completed a thirty-six hour march in heat and heavy rain, with only four hours rest and a sharp skirmish in the village of Strada on the way. At nightfall the Argylls attacked Vaiano and were engaged until midnight in close fighting among the scattered houses and gardens on the outskirts of the town. At 2am an enemy counter-attack over-ran their outlying platoon position, forcing the Argylls to withdraw. Casualties were two men killed, sixteen wounded and thirty-six missing. The village was held by a full battalion, who put up the stiffest resistance since Alatri.

Conditions within Vaiano are graphically described in *The Trasimene Line:*
To the dismay of the villagers from their refuge in the *cantine* below the *palazzo* in the village square or in the hideouts in the steep olive groves leading down to Lake Chiusi, they heard the campanile of their church crashing down. Those who ventured out saw burnt out tanks belonging to the Wiltshire Yeomanry lining the road which comes into the village from Villastrada.

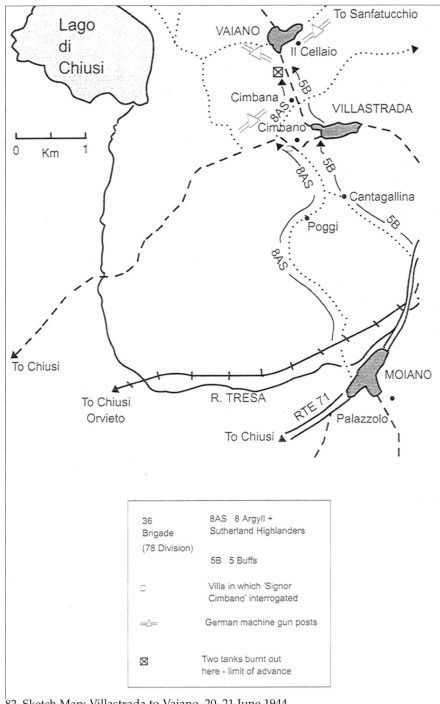

82. Sketch Map: Villastrada to Vaiano, 20–21 June 1944.

From the same source Colonel John Horsfall of the London Irish Rifles describes events to his flank:

That evening (20 June) the Argylls carried Villastrada several miles away on our left and pushing further on, got into Vaiano a mile east of Lake Chiusi. Here in the darkness they were heavily counter attacked, and by the time the night was out the Argylls were driven from the place with heavy loss, including regrettably, a good many prisoners.

Brigadier James,[27] who commanded 36th Infantry Brigade remained undismayed by the setback, though not realising its significance. The following day (21 June), he unleashed the Buffs against this key position – they too were savagely handled and sent back reeling. 36th Brigade in a day and a half's heavy fighting had come to a dead stop.

At this stage 36th Infantry Brigade were relieved by 28th Infantry Brigade, whose leading troops were in sight now of Lake Trasimene, vast and placid and surrounded by thickly wooded slopes. Orders had been received for 78th division to be withdrawn from the line and to go to Egypt for a rest. The advance party were already on their way. But now that the enemy had settled itself strongly south of the lake, it was clear that the Division had some fighting to do before it could leave the line.

As the next actions did not involve John's Brigade, we shall pass them by, save to say that they centred on the villages of San Fatucchio and Pucciarelli. Both were strongly held and put up fierce resistance while attacks and counter-attacks swung both ways during the next few days until San Fatucchio was finally secured.

It then became the Eighth Army's task to attack and break through past Lake Trasimene. 78th Division was to advance along the western shore of the lake, with 4th British Division on their left while further left the South Africans were having a hard battle for Chiusi.

The attack opened on 24 June with an artillery concentration. The Irish Brigade was to take Pescia and Ranciano, both just south of the River Pescia and inland from the lake. While at this time of year this tiny river was no more than a ditch, it was still an effective anti-tank obstacle with enemy dug in on its far bank. The actual crossing was down to 36th Brigade which was to pass through the Irish Brigade, once both villages had been secured. 11 Infantry Brigade was to the right along the lake shore.

At 5.30 am on 24 June the Irish Brigade supported by 11th Canadian Armoured Regiment attacked and after slow hard fighting had established a company in each village by late afternoon. Then at 6 pm the Buffs, at the head of 36th Infantry Brigade, came through, crossed the stream and started

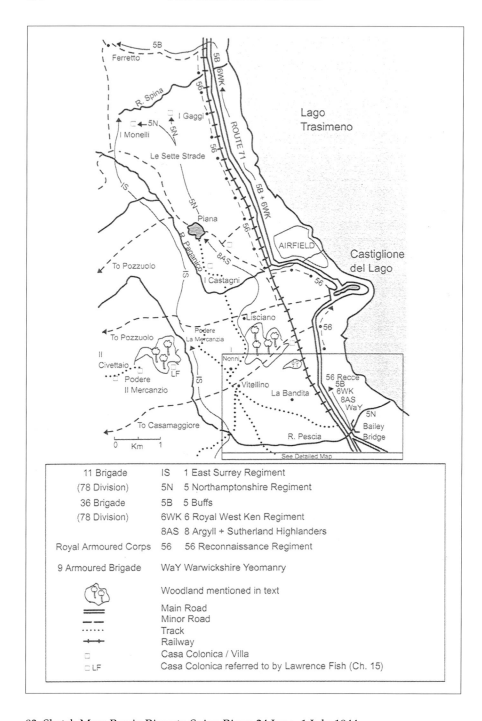

11 Brigade	IS	1 East Surrey Regiment
(78 Division)	5N	5 Northamptonshire Regiment
36 Brigade	5B	5 Buffs
(78 Division)	6WK	6 Royal West Ken Regiment
	8AS	8 Argyll + Sutherland Highlanders
Royal Armoured Corps	56	56 Reconnaissance Regiment
9 Armoured Brigade	WaY	Warwickshire Yeomanry

Woodland mentioned in text
═══ Main Road
── Minor Road
...... Track
┼─┼─┼ Railway
☐ Casa Colonica / Villa
☐ LF Casa Colonica referred to by Lawrence Fish (Ch. 15)

83. Sketch Map: Pescia River to Spina River, 24 June–1 July 1944.

digging themselves into a small bridgehead. The Wiltshire Yeomanry's tanks had been unable to make the crossing.

There was heavy shelling of the Buffs in the bridgehead, of the Royal West Kents on the nearside of the stream and of the Sappers erecting a Bailley bridge. Heavy rain plus the failure of the tanks to make the crossing slowed down operations that night. The German shelling seemed to be directed from OPs at Castiglione del Lago, a village on a small promontory jutting into the lake further north.

25 and 26 June 1944

At seven next morning, 25 June, the Royal West Kents crossed the Bailley bridge which had been completed under heavy shelling in the rain. The Argylls and the Northamptons followed. The crossing was hazardous and the shelling was among the heaviest which the Division had experienced. On the far side, fighting was bitter and all the battalions suffered many casualties. The Royal West Kents, who had passed through the Buffs during the morning, had been unable to enter Castiglione del Lago due to heavy mortar and machine gun fire. After crossing the Pescia, the Northamptons occupied some houses where they were shelled and mortared all day and all night and were forced to withdraw.

John's last letter to Anne was written on 25 June during his Brigade's battle for Castiglione del Lago and after a period of intense activity for his Brigade since 18 June. Kesselring's strong defence of the Albert Line was taking a toll on a Brigade which was overdue some rest in Egypt, but could not yet get away. Not only does he admit being tired but it was written in pencil and incorrectly numbered. Nevertheless it was typically reassuring and upbeat.

Letter 100 P27213 Brig J G James DSO
June 25 1944 HQ 36 Inf Bde
My Darling Anne
— Am so sorry that I haven't written since letter 100 on 16 June but have been in the thick of things & frightfully busy! You understand I'm sure my darling. I am very fit & well but dirty & tired — but I hope to put both of the latter right shortly!
I loved your letter 117 my darling — thank you so much, my darling.
It is a nuisance about David's tonsils — I leave all the arrangements to you, my darling, with complete confidence. I think it's so wonderful the way you organise & arrange things. I'm sure once they're 'out,' he will fill out a great deal! Bless him.
Simply must off — excuse haste. You are always in my thoughts as you know.

God bless for always darling.
Ever your loving
John
     xxxxx

The following paragraph is extracted verbatim from page 150 of *Algiers to Austria. A History of the 78th Division during the Second World War:*

That night two Italians volunteered to reconnoitre Castiglione del Lago. They set off at midnight and returned at 3 am to report that there were only patrols in the town, not a full occupying force, although there was a battery of guns in action. But 36th Brigade was not to reach Castiglione yet: they held their ground throughout the next day while the other two brigades straightened the line to the rear. The Germans were reported to be reinforcing and had brought over the 104 Panzer Grenadier Regiment from Perugia. The Argylls were on the left, furthest from the lake, and that day suffered nine casualties from shelling. Just behind them and on the right the Royal West Kents were particularly heavily shelled and mortared: their considerable casualties on 26th June included Brigadier James, commanding 36th Infantry Brigade, killed by gunfire ahead of the Royal West Kents' positions. He had been commanding the Brigade since April and was succeeded by Brigadier Packard DSO, who had been commanding the Divisional Artillery... .

An extract from the *War Diaries of the 78th Division and 36th Infantry Brigade* are a little more detailed:

In the course of operations to enlarge a bridgehead over the River Pescia, Brigadier James was killed by an unlucky shell from a self propelled German 88 mm gun while carrying out a reconnaissance in his jeep in the forward area of the Royal West Kents. His death occurred at 9.15am on 26th June 1944.

The following two paragraphs are extracted verbatim from page 150 of *Alexander's Generals, The Italian Campaign 1944–1945* by Gregory Blaxland.

That evening a sudden thunderstorm gave cover and impetus to a dashing crossing of the little River Pescia made by the Buffs (The Royal West Kents), of 36th Brigade, under the inspiration of a veteran company commander. They took a Tiger tank, a gun with its team of horses, and 53 prisoners, which latter score lifted the division's total to over 250 since the start of the Irish attack.

The fact that the Buffs were left in isolation through bridging difficulties and yet were not dislodged, emphasised the extent of the enemy's

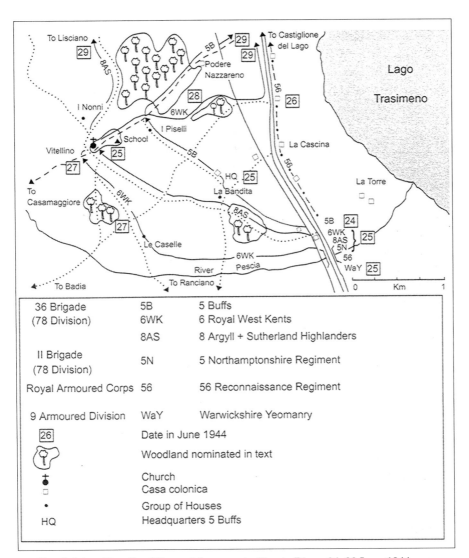

84. Sketch Map: Details of Troop Movements, Pescia River, 24–29 June 1944.

disorder. The backbone of the Trasimene line had been broken, and although further rainstorms aggravated problems of exploitation, and although Brigadier James, of 36th Brigade, met death through inadvertently driving past his forward troops, the advance chugged back into general motion, with the 4th Division making better progress along the range of hills between the main roads, the South Africans swooping onwards on finding Chiusi abandoned, and 56th Recce, of 78th Division, gaining passage round the northern shore of the lake, were at Tuoro on

85. Investiture at Buckingham Palace for John's DSO on 17 July 1945. L to R; David, Anne, Davina and Trill (John's twin).

July 3rd when they met the King's Dragoon Guards, coming from the other side.'

After becoming a soldier myself and gaining some understanding of battlefield tactics, I harboured a suspicion – occasionally resentfully – that my father may have been too far forward at the time. Some sixty years on from 1944, my recent researches seem to confirm my earlier suspicion. But this sad discovery so aptly described, also shows that in the heat of battle, while striving to exploit a crucial break in the enemy's defences in appalling weather, just how easy it is for a Brigade Commander to press forward too far. Whether it was radio failure, a wrong grid reference, sheer determination to grasp the initiative, a misjudgement or as the *War Diaries* imply sheer bad luck, we shall never really know. However it was typical of him to wish to lead from the front; it was his Brigade that broke through Kesselring's Trasimene Line.

Orvieto Cemetery

John was laid to rest in Orvieto Cemetery, which is a little distance south of

86. Oil portrait of Brigadier John Gwynne-James DSO.

the town. It is a small and lovingly cared for cemetery in a peaceful rural setting. Each grave stone has its own flowers tended with great care. A small brook and nearby farm with quacking ducks brings life to this most intimate and unforgettable resting place.

Orvieto, perched on its high rock – declared an open city in 1944 – stands sentinel. The gold mosaic front to her magnificent Cathedral glinting proudly in the evening sun dominates the town square. It is surely a time to sample a bottle of Orvieto Classico Secco; to take in the scenery of this beautiful country, yet to reflect on the terrain over which the Allies fought from the stalemate in December 1943 until ultimate victory in Italy on 2 May 1945.

Climate and terrain

The savage severity of the winter of 1943/4 spent either south of Cassino or in the Anzio beachhead must have seemed a depressing foretaste of an endless succession of obstacles which favoured the defender. North of the apparently impenetrable fortress of Cassino rises the massif of Monte Cairo leading to the rugged mountains of the Abruzzi, which were considered too difficult terrain in which to deploy large forces. Level with Rome, the Appenines stretch up Italy's spine for a further three hundred miles before dropping to the Po valley south of Milan. At every stage along this invariably muddy way there were dominating hills, woods or towns to clear and rivers to cross. Add the skilful resistance of the Germans using fiendish demolitions and fiercely fought rearguard actions to cover their withdrawal to the next main defensive line and you get some idea of the bravery and stamina required. While the Allies enjoyed air and sea superiority throughout, the relative strengths of respective armies were broadly similar.

Were the sacrifices and suffering in Italy justified?

To answer this question we need to understand the Allied strategy in Europe and on the Russian front. Championed by Winston Churchill and accepted by Franklin Roosevelt, it was to attack the Axis underbelly. This would force Hitler to fight simultaneously on three fronts – firstly on two – North Africa/Italy and the Russian front. Then with Germany overstretched to prize open a third – in North West Europe.

The Allied victory in North Africa in May 1943 was followed by assault landings on Pantelleria in June and on Sicily in July. The Allied victory in Sicily knocked Italy out of the war and led to their surrender in early September. This left their country to become a battle ground between the Germans and the Allies until May 1945.

87. John's grave in the
Commonwealth Cemetery at
Orvieto, Italy.

88. Orvieto Cathedral town, 1959.

By January 1944, and despite Salerno, Cassino and Anzio, the focus of the war had switched to preparations for D Day in North West Europe. It is in the context of the Normandy Landings on 6 June 1944 leading to ultimate victory, that we can try to measure the impact of the Italian Campaign in drawing away German Divisions from the Western and Eastern fronts.

> March 1944 3rd Battle of Cassino
> 21 Allied Divisions versus 22 German Divisions
> 11 May 1944 Gustav Line
> 25 Allied Divisions versus 23 German Divisions
> August 1944 Gothic Line
> 20 Allied Divisions versus 26 German Divisions
> 9 April 1945 Final Offensive
> 17 Allied Divisions versus 20 German Divisions

It was, of course, events on the Western and Eastern fronts that decided the issue. But had the Germans been able to deploy their 20–26 Divisions against the D Day landings and during the subsequent offensive, there could have been a very different outcome in Northern Europe in 1944/45. The brutal, bitter and hard fought campaign in Italy was justified and made this crucial difference. The War in Italy 1943–1945 was a vital contribution to Victory in Europe.

Appendices

1 Statement of Service.
2. Citation for the Award of the Distinguished Service Order to T/Lt Col J G James 1 KSLI for action on 24 April 1943.
3. Letter dated 11 February 1944 to Major General W R C Penney, CBE, DSO, MC Commanding General 1st British Division from Major General John P Lucas, United States Army, Commanding VI Corps (overmarked by JGJ).
4. Letter dated 20 May 1944 to Brigade Commander, 36th Infantry Brigade from Major General C F Keightley, CBE, OBE General officer Commanding 78th Division (overmarked by JGJ).
5. Congratulatory Message dated 7 June 1944 to all Units from Major General C F Keightley, CBE, OBE General Officer Commanding 78th Division.

Appendix 1: Statement of Service

1 September 1921 to 12 July 1923	Cadet at Royal Military College, Sandhurst
30 August 1923	Second Lieutenant, 2nd Battalion, King's Shropshire Light Infantry at Tidworth
22 February 1924	Embarked at Tilbury on SS *Kaiser-i-Hind* en route to join 1st Battalion, King's Shropshire Light Infantry in India
14 March 1924	Disembarked Bombay. Joined 1st Battalion, King's Shropshire Light Infantry in Poona
30 August 1925	Promoted to Lieutenant, 1st Battalion, King's Shropshire Light Infantry in Poona
10 March 1927	Embarked at Bombay for 8 months leave from Dinapore
27 October 1927	Disembarked at Bombay from SS *City of Nagpur* to rejoin 1st Battalion, King's Shropshire Light Infantry in Dinapore
26 January 1929	Embarked at Karachi on HT *Nevassa* on transfer to UK as Class A Invalid from Razmak
13 August 1929	Posted to Regimental Depot, King's Shropshire Light Infantry at Shrewsbury
23 September 1931	Embarked at Southampton on HT *Somersetshire* on posting to 1st Battalion, King's Shropshire Light Infantry in India
19 October 1931	Disembarked at Karachi from HT *Somersetshire* to rejoin 1st Battalion, King's Shropshire Light Infantry at Gharial
11 August 1932	Embarked at Bombay on SS *Victoria* for UK
11 October 1932	Posted to 2nd Battalion, King's Shropshire Light Infantry in Colchester
July & August 1933	Staff Captain, 160th Infantry Brigade in Tenby
1 October 1933 to 3 January 1935	Staff Captain, 11th Infantry Brigade in Colchester
4 April 1935	Promoted to Captain, 2nd Battalion, King's Shropshire Light Infantry in Colchester
16 July 1935 to 10 December 1938	Appointed Adjutant, 2nd Battalion, King's Shropshire Light Infantry in Pembroke Dock
23 January 1939	Staff Captain, 3rd Infantry Brigade at Bordon
24 September 1939	Embarked at Southampton for France
26 December 1939	Disembarked at Southampton from France to join as

	Student at Staff College, Camberley
27 May 1940	Appointed General Staff Officer Grade 3, 4th Division and embarked for France
28 May 1940 to 18 June 1940	Served with Beauman Division as Assistant Brigade Major and disembarked from France with British Expeditionary Force
24 June 1940	Posted to Infantry Training Centre, Shrewsbury
26 June 1940	Posted as Second in Command 5th Battalion, King's Shropshire Light Infantry in Liverpool
3 July 1940	Promoted Major
22 July 1940	Posted General Staff Officer Grade 2 (Civ) 6th Corps in Ireland
22 October 1940 to 11 July 1941	Appointed Instructor (GSO2) at Senior Officers School at Devizes as Local Lieutenant Colonel
11 July 1941	Posted to Infantry Training Centre, Shrewsbury
6 August 1941	Appointed General Staff Officer Grade 1, North Wales Area and Acting Lieutenant Colonel at Shrewsbury
1 July 1942	Appointed to Command 1st Battalion, King's Shropshire Light Infantry in Great Yarmouth
28 February 1943	Embarked at Glasgow with 1st Battalion, part of 3rd Infantry Brigade, 1st Division and landed in North Africa, Operation Torch
6 July 1943	Awarded the Distinguished Service Order for his Leadership and Gallantry on 24 April 1943
30 April 1943	Appointed to Command 3rd Infantry Brigade, 1st Division in North Africa as Brigadier
10 June 1943	Commanded the Assault Landing by 3rd Infantry Brigade at Island of Pantelleria
22 January to 7 March 1944	Commanded 3rd Infantry Brigade during Assault Landing at Anzio and during subsequent fighting in the Anzio Beachhead
April 1944	Transferred to Command 36th Infantry Brigade, 78th Division.
18 May 1944	Fourth Battle of Cassino
26 June 1944	Killed in Action near Lake Trasimene, Perugia

Appendix 2

Citation for the Award of the Distinguished Service Order to T/Lt Col J G James 1 KSLI for action on 24 April 1943

CITATION.

T/Lt.Col. J.G. JAMES (27213) - 1 K.S.L.I.
(now Brigadier).

RECEIVED
8 DEC 19-4
ACCOUNTS

By Bde Comd.

In the afternoon of 24 Apr 43, Lt.Col.J.G.James commanded 1 K.S.L.I. in the attack on Pt.170. This attack was put in against fierce enemy opposition and was entirely successful though not without loss. During the night successful exploitation was carried out to Pt.168. Throughout the attack,Lt.Col.J.G.JAMES showed outstanding qualitites of determination and initiative. His energy and disregard for his own personal safety resulted in his being able to make quick and accurate decisions which ensured the complete success of this most vital operation. The high quality and achievement of the Battalion in recent operations has been exemplified in the performance of its Commanding Officer, Lt.Col. J.G. JAMES.

-o-o-o-o-o-o-o-o-o-o-

By Divisional Commander.

A great natural leader, who, on this occasion, made a success of a most difficult operation by his personal bravery, which he has displayed again and again on subsequent occasions.

-o-o-o-o-o-o-o-o-o-o-

Appendix 3

Letter dated 11 February 1944 to Major General W R C Penney, CBE, DSO, MC Commanding General 1st British Division from Major General John P Lucas, United States Army, Commanding VI Corps (overmarked by JGJ)

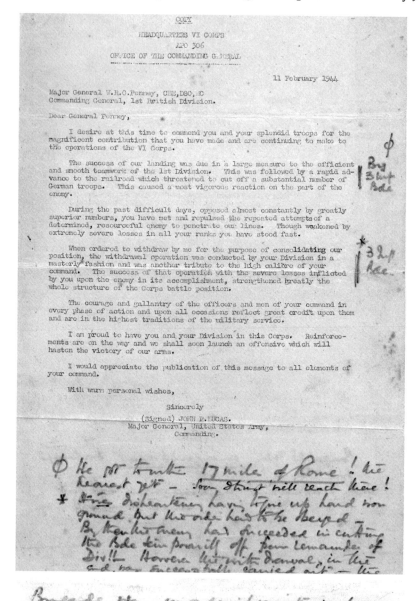

Appendix 4

Letter dated 20 May 1944 to Brigade Commander, 36th Infantry Brigade
from Major General C F Keightley, CBE, OBE
General Officer Commanding 78th Division (overmarked by JGJ)

Copy of a Personal Message from the G.O.C. 78 Division,
Maj.-Gen C.F. Keightley, C.B., O.B.E., to the Bde Commander, 36 Bde.

- -

In the Field.

20 May 44.
- - - - -

The Commander-in-Chief, General Alexander, and the Army Commander, have both sent their personal congratulations to the Division in its fine achievements during the last few days.

I endorse these congratulations with all my heart.

Your Bde had the hardest task of any in the Division, and the results were in keeping with the high traditions of each Bn.

Your long approach march through the night was a fine achievement in itself, and Bns arriving at the end of it, ready to attack, was splendid.

Big chances come very seldom in war, and the rapid advance of this Division did give the chance of breaking the Adolf Hitler line before it was properly manned.   This chance had to be taken before the next day if it was to succeed.   There was no other way to seize this chance than to attack, and your Bde was the only one so placed to reach it in time.

Your attack was well planned and brilliantly and gallantly executed. The Buffs, with the exposed right flank and handicapped by the loss of tanks, and the Argylls difficult country on the left, made obstacles which demanded initiative on the part of leaders and steadfastness on the part of the men.
The 6 Royal West Kents had the longest and hardest march of all, and were then subjected to shelling and mortaring.   They did not get the chance of exploitation, but if the spirit of the whole Bn was that of the few men I spoke to during the attack, they would have won any objective you had been told to seize.

In spite of very heavy mortaring and shelling those men who failed this great Divisional team of ours were few.   This is an indication of a high spirit in Bns, and I will see to it that those who run the most risks and still stick it in our battles get the consideration they have earned.

During the last 10 days this Division formed the left pincer in the attack on Cassino and the Monastery, and our successful and rapid advance was largely responsible for its capture.

During this advance we have :-
    Captured over 400 prisoners.
    Killed or wounded over 300 enemy.
    Knocked out or captured over 40 enemy tanks or S.P. guns.
    Captured a considerable amount of equipment.
In addition to this, it can only be guessed what effect this advance had on loosening up the French and Polish fronts by necessitating the rapid removal of reserves from their fronts to deal with our threat.

Such actions all help to hasten the end of the war, and all who have been through them may justly feel proud of the part they have played whatever that part may have been.

Appendix 5

Congratulatory Message dated 7 June 1944 to all Units from Major General C F Keightley, CBE, OBE General Officer Commanding 78th

SUBJECT :- Congratulatory Message.

Main HQ 78 Div.

113/309/G.

Lists 'A', 'B' and 'C' (Down to Units).

7 Jun 44.

The following is an extract from a letter received by me from the Army Commander, Lieut-Gen Sir Oliver W.H. Leese, Bt, KCB, CBE, DSO.

" Now that the 78th Division is out of the line, I should like to send my best congratulations on the tremendous energy and drive your Division showed throughout its successive fights.

The excellent training of the Division has more than proved itself on the day. Its excellent attacks towards Highway Six, supported by tanks and artillery, were admirably organised and carried out and led decisively to the fall of Cassino and the Monastery Hill.

I am very grateful for the quick contact your troops gained along the Hitler Line, and for your flank march from Arce, as well as the general speed of movement achieved. The many physical difficulties of the ground were admirably overcome and throughout the hard fighting in the mountains the spirit and toughness of the troops was beyond praise.

All this I expected from the great traditions of your Division with its fine record in North Africa, Sicily and Eastern Italy. I well realise the hard and difficult fighting the Division had all through the winter and the severe casualties suffered in those months. To have succeeded soon after in the hard fought actions of the last three weeks is a great achievement and reflects the greatest credit on all ranks.

I am seeing to it that good accounts of the deeds of individual Regiments appear in the papers at home.

My personal congratulations and heartfelt thanks to yourself and your fine Division. "

In passing on this message just after the opening of the Western Front I would add one thing.

You may with every reason feel that your hard and gallant fighting has made the task of the troops there more certain of success.

The Allied Armies in Italy have disposed of some 50,000 enemy in four weeks. And the pursuit still continues. The enemy has moved some six reserve Divisions, some of which have already been annihilated.

If we can keep him on the run we shall have secured another victory as great as North Africa or Stalingrad.

In the Field.

Maj.-Gen.,
Comd.

Family Recollections

How the War curtailed recollections of him

Sadly my recollections of my father are limited because I was only two when the war started in September 1939. Although I had just turned seven when he was killed on 26 June 1944, the war had kept him away from us for much of the intervening four and three quarter years. Even so, I nevertheless have recollections of a very loving man who was always full of fun.

At the outbreak of war in September 1939 he was in France for three months and for three weeks at Dunkirk in 1940, when he was declared missing. From the moment he took over command of the 1st Battalion, The King's Shropshire Light Infantry on 1 July 1942 his family had to take second place. His priority was to train his battalion to peak fitness to fight the Germans and Italians in North Africa. Because the battalion was based at Great Yarmouth and trained at Callander in Scotland, our parents decided we should continue to live at Littlegates, 2 Bourne Grove Close, Farnham, Surrey, where they had been since he had been stationed at Bordon. When he embarked from Glasgow for North Africa on 28 February 1943, our mother was thirty eight, Davina was eight and I was five. We would not see him again. As Davina was two and a half years older, her recollections of our father are more vivid than mine.

John was only forty years old and just three weeks from promotion to Major General when he was killed. His 101 letters home to our mother were loving, upbeat and seemed to portray someone who was in his element when in command. Nevertheless they did reveal a deep tiredness towards the end and a longing for the war to end.

Being a natural leader, he relished the opportunities which came with becoming one of the younger Brigadiers in the British Army at the time. His success as a battlefield commander was due to a combination of sound judgement, calmness under pressure, bravery and good timing. Yet his letters home seemed to sense that while he had been fortunate to be at the right place at the right time, his consequent prolonged absence placed unrelenting strain on our mother. His expression of complete confidence in her judgement and ability to manage all home matters must have been a huge encouragement to her.

From January 1944 the focus of world attention had switched to England and the steady build up in preparations for the Allied Invasion of Northern Europe. By the fall of Rome on 4 June, Operation Overlord was ready for launch amid tight security on where the landings would take place. Fairly soon after this vast and brilliantly executed assault landing on the Normandy beaches on 6 June 1944, radio bulletins were reporting successful breakouts from all five Allied beachheads. After nearly five years of warfare against Germany there was now, at last, a real prospect of ultimate victory in Europe. But how long would this take?

The Allies now concentrated their resources to drive back Hitler's Axis Forces into the heart of Germany. Inevitably reports from Italy, Burma and the Pacific became back page items in the newspapers.

However, it was precisely at this time of encouraging news from Normandy that our mother received her dreaded telegram from the War Office that John had been killed in action. To then learn that her husband's best friend, Jack Maurice had also been killed while commanding 2nd Battalion the King's Shropshire Light Infantry near Caen one month after D Day, must have been the final straw.

Coming to terms with loss

As an utterly devastated and frightened 39 year old widow, she first had to steel herself to tell her two children the heart breaking news that their father had been killed in action.

Being nine and seven years old respectively, she knew that we were at an impressionable age so this had to be done as best she could in the circumstances. She took us up to her bedroom, where she sat up against the bed-head inviting us to do the same on either side of her. Then putting her arms around us, she said she had some bad news to tell us. With great love and scarcely concealed emotion she told us that our father had been killed fighting in Italy. That he would always love us and that after a good cry we must be brave too, as he would have wished us to be.

Naturally she then had the wretched task of telling other members of the James family in Hereford and of course her own parents in Salisbury. Davina remembers the prompt arrival of 'Grannie and Grandpa Salisbury' to comfort us. Just as they were driving up the lane to park outside, Davina remembers our mother turning to her and saying 'Do I look if I have been crying?' Later she remembers 'Grannie and Grandpa Hereford' suggesting that we should all live in Hereford for a while. Despite this kind offer and considerable pressure to do so, our mother's sense of independence prevailed and we remained at Littlegates.

Tina, my cousin felt the loss of her younger brother John acutely for, just like the rest of the family, it brought back memories of Eric's death in 1916. Her soldier husband Tony O'Carroll Scott, who was fighting in Burma at the time, wrote home to console her:

Grieve not for him. Grieve for yourself.
You are right – you never will see him again: you will never feel the clasp of his

hand. BUT you will always see his face as it was: see his smile as it was: hear
his great laugh as it was. And AS IT WAS WHEN HE WAS <u>YOUNG</u>.
Even when you are an old woman you will know him still as in youth. You
will never remember him as a querulous old gentleman – bit of a bore, bit of a
bear, all Uncle Willyish – Because he never lived to be that. Always will he
remain to you a youth.
A gay mocking daring youth. On the top of his form until – flick, out.
Not a bad way to go Matewoman! Not a bad way to leave a memory
behind one.

Sixty years later it is impossible to remember how we took this news
other than perhaps in disbelief. Like all families we shared our grief and
helped each other as best we could. For some time I remember praying
that there had been a mistake and that he would walk in smiling and
hug us all.

This hope finally crashed when several weeks later his trunk containing
his uniform and belongings arrived. We remember this being a totally
wretched time, particularly for our mother who was at last incapable of
containing her grief.

Next, like countless other war widows, she had to find the resolve to face
the prospect of bringing up her children alone. Drawing strongly on a
mother's natural instinct to love and protect her children, whatever the
circumstances, she resolved to lead her family out of despair and to take
every step possible to assure their future happiness.

After all, this is what both our parents had discussed earlier and agreed
between them in the event of either of them being killed. However, dwelling
on such dark possibilities during their precious time together would have
served little purpose, other than to show mutual love and support for any
future tragedy which might strike.

This understanding was extremely important, as was the example of
bravery and resolve of other families who had already suffered in this way.
Yet actually to do what is necessary is another matter altogether. To our
mother's enormous credit she never seemed to waver.

Just to compound her grief at the time, although on reflection this may
have helped her, there were two practical matters which needed to be
addressed straight away. The first related to my health as a seven year old.
Like many youngsters of my age I had been very susceptible to colds,
coughs and bronchial infections and it had been suggested by Doctor Griffin
that I would benefit if my tonsils and adenoids were removed. This subject
had been foremost in correspondence between our parents and our mother
was waiting for his blessing by letter from Italy, when she had received her

telegram from the War Office. Initially she could not face the prospect of me going into hospital at this time and without his blessing so she understandably cancelled these plans. A week or so later she received his last two letters, the second giving her his blessing and suggesting that she should go ahead and follow Doctor Griffin's advice. With a heavy heart she gave Doctor Griffin her permission to proceed.

The second matter related to their plans for me to start at Heatherdown (Preparatory) School at Ascot as a boarder in September 1944, aged seven and a quarter. Now that father had been killed, my mother saw no prospect of being able to afford the school fees of £60 per term. She telephoned the Headmaster, Charles Warner to cancel my entry and explained what had happened. When Charles Warner heard my mother's reasons for doing so, he immediately reassured her saying 'Of course, we shall be delighted to have David at Heatherdown anyway. Do not concern yourself about the fees'. Any reservations she may have had about my leaving home at this difficult time were dispelled by an exasperated and tactless remark of mine, 'I'm the only man now that Daddy has been killed – even the hens are girls!' She was also reassured to hear that there were other boys who had lost their fathers who were at the school and another was starting in September. This typical understanding and generous offer by Charles Warner lifted a cloud of uncertainty and made it possible after all to stick to their original plan. This outcome enabled me to enjoy a happy and excellent early education at Heatherdown for the next five years for a fee of £10 per term.

This generation responded magnificently to the losses and deprivation which war spread so far and wide. It was as if their parents had set a stoic example during the horrific losses of the First War and that no less could be expected of them in another. Perhaps this time they helped each other more naturally and openly than before. Time and again people returned kindnesses which helped to build a spirit of shared determination to survive, to make the best of a bad deal, to show some spirit and to move on.

Family recollections of my father

Now that sixty years have elapsed since my father was killed in 1944 there are only three living members of the family who remember him. His niece June Robertson (now 76), his daughter, Davina Vickers (now 70) and myself (just 68). For reasons explained earlier none of us possess vivid memories of him, but each of us has our own enduring recollections. By readily agreeing to share these, it has enabled me to sketch an outline of the type of man he was.

When June, as a small girl, stayed at Aylestone Hill, Hereford, the James Family home, she could at any time see up to four Uncles and two Aunts. She called the youngest, my father, her 'uncomfy Uncle'. This was not that he was ever unkind, but just that 'he would always carry me under his arm like a rugger ball'.

'He would also tease me unmercifully and call me 'gorse bush' because of my hair and 'letterbox' because of my mouth. He was much loved and full of fun. On one occasion when waiting for some time outside the YWCA where his mother was attending a meeting, he sent in a message 'Please tell Mrs James, her house is on fire!'

On another occasion he visited the jewellers in Hereford and persuaded the pretty girl behind the counter to get every single clock out of the cabinet. He then with a twinkle helped her put them all back. He went in to the Post Office to buy a stamp. Pointing to one in the middle of a large sheet, he said '*That* one, please!' He was also infinitely kind and his elder sister Tina (June's mother), who shared with her younger brother a love of games, once saw him carrying the bags of an old tramp.

Stories like these help to complete the jig saw, just as our mother used to recall many happy incidents they shared. As we grew up Davina and I relished these as they helped us to know our father better. Also over the course of many years we were delighted to meet those who had known him and quizzed them enthusiastically. This helped us to highlight certain aspects of his personality and to confirm our pride in him.

In our very early years Davina and I remember our mother and he taking it in turns to read to us at bedtime. Excited anticipation lead to delight and gradual sleepiness as favourites of the time, *Little Black Sambo, Little Lord Fontleroy* and *Rumple Stiltskin* were read with flair. We joined in with gusto during the best bits. Another favourite of the time was *Let me tell you...* which were rhymes by Ursula Bloom illustrated by Dora Shackell. One of these was about a rather obnoxious little boy called 'Percy Polite, a child who was always right.'

I also particularly remember asking my father once again to read about the elephants. With his bowed head and extending his arms towards the floor, he would mimmick how they go to sleep standing up, swaying their head and trunk from side to side. That they have small eyes, big ears, huge tusks but normally were gentle creatures who never forget, made them our favourite animal. Father would recount how Hannibal employed them with his army in the Alps. How the soldiers painted the elephants' hind quarters with huge frightening faces. How they reversed them up to the crest of hills to confuse, frighten and rout larger armies.

Davina can remember her Daddy shinning up a drainpipe at 'the Hill', the family home in Hereford. She also remembers an episode during our time in Pembroke Dock when John was Adjutant to Lieutenant-Colonel Dix-Perkin. When her Daddy was struggling to take off his highly polished riding boots in the nursery at the end of the day, he was often heard to mutter, 'That bloody man!' (Dix-Perkin). This clearly stuck in Davina's mind. When introduced to the Commanding Officer shortly before a dinner party in his honour, to say goodnight before going upstairs to bed, with a smile she declared 'Hullo, bloody man!' Much to everyone's relief Dix-Perkin laughed the loudest of all. I was too young to know what all the fuss was about.

Davina also remembers her Daddy and his batman, Jack O'Shea, teaching her how to do the Lambeth Walk. This was acted to the full and always ended with a competition as to who could shout the loudest 'Oi'. She also remembers being enchanted by the sight of her mother and father in full evening dress before going to Hunt Balls. She even remembers that her mother would have her hair done at Vasco's and use Elizabeth Arden orange skin food. Father often gave her Chanel No 5.

Much later on his return from Dunkirk when he had been declared 'missing', he rang home to tell us that he was alive, well and was heading home. When he arrived at Littlegates there was much excitement as he muddied and exhausted hugged us all. He removed his revolver from his holster, extracted the bullets and sat down with us at the dining room table for tea. Drawing the bread board nearer, he then cut the loaf in half, pushed one half towards us and proceeded to demolish the other.

Both of our parents were keen on eggs for breakfast, which during wartime rationing were difficult to come by. Dried eggs were tasteless and needed syrup of figs to shift. Not only did they install some Rhode Island Red and Black Leghorn chickens in the garden at Littlegates, but throughout the North African and Italian Campaigns my father kept a cockerel and a couple of chickens in his Jeep trailer. They were tied to his tent pole at night.

Later Reflections
Every family responds differently to loss and we recall some relief when mother decided to dispose of virtually all father's uniform save for his Brigadier's forage cap, red flashes and badges of rank. Occasionally I would open his zinc lined trunk to look at these with awe. Also in the trunk was his .45 service revolver. Using two fingers I could just pull the trigger!

Naturally we wanted to know how father had been killed. Some time later Major Ernest Dynes, his Brigade Major came to Littlegates to tell us what had happened. As I recall, he had just been released from hospital and walked with a limp, having been severely wounded in the same action.

With great gentleness, he explained that father, he, a signaller and driver had been travelling together in a jeep near Lake Trasimene. The Germans were holding this line strongly and there was a need to break the stalemate.

(The pennant on the Brigadier's jeep may have been spotted by a German Observation Post). Suddenly they came under extremely accurate artillery fire. They scrambled out of the jeep to take cover in the ditch by the side of the road. As father put his head up to check that the others had reached cover, his jeep received a direct hit and father was instantly killed. He would have known no pain.

Occasionally father would send individual postcards to Davina and I with encouraging and loving messages, much as Eric had done from the trenches during the First War to his brothers and sisters. Davina recalls that many of her cards were of Spitfires. For many years, up until it finally disintegrated, I kept the last postcard he wrote to me inside my wallet. This was probably from Rome after its fall to Lieutenant General Mark Clark's US 5th Army. The picture was of a coloured sketch of a beach scene in poor weather. It portrayed a very large woman on a deckchair alongside her spindly, rather disconsolate husband. The rhyme underneath read:

'What's the use of looking glum?
It only adds to sorrow
The sun shone on the world before,
It might come back tomorrow!'

On the back he had written some message, and ended up saying 'Remember to take care of Mummy'. As this was my last word from him, this request, which had been written innocently enough at the time, assumed great significance to me, when he was killed. Although I was younger than my sister, Davina, I somehow felt that it was up to me, 'the man', to do exactly what father had asked. This responsibility may have rested rather heavily on a seven year old. In practice it never really left me. On the eve of the fifty-seventh anniversary of his death, my mother turned to me from her hospital bed and asked 'What is the date?' By then ninety six years of age and increasingly frail following a bad fall, she seemed content to hear that the next day would be 26 June (2001). When she died two days later, we felt some comfort from knowing that we had done our best to carry out his wishes.

CHAPTER 5
Reflections

WE CAN ASSUME that nobody alive today will remember Eric, but there are some who still remember Henry and John. These few and the more senior members of our family still treasure their recollections. As I now have the unique advantage of my researches for this book to call upon, it seems to me that this tribute would not be complete without endeavouring to summarise the differing personalities of all three brothers. There is of course an inherent danger of filling the gaps in my personal knowledge by brush stroking in my own perceptions of each personality. This may be so, but I still believe my portrayals will be very close to the kind of men they were.

*   *   *

Eric was a good looking, tall, athletic and fine principled young man. He had great charm and a quiet presence and a ready smile which won him friends and admirers. For someone still young he seemed to have an inner strength, probably based on his belief in God, acquired through the example of his parents. By nature he was tactful and diplomatic and avoided unnecessary confrontation, unless there was no other alternative. He had a good intellect, was well organised and good manager of people. He was determined and had stamina in the face of adversity. He was a talented cricketer, useful at rugby and a good rifle shot, but above all else he was a lover of animals and particularly horses. He was happiest in the country-side riding a horse preferably in wide open spaces. He had a delightful sense of humour and was much interested and greatly encouraged his brothers and sisters in all their exploits.

Had he escaped the war unscathed, in all probability he would have returned to Oriel College, Oxford to complete his studies. There is no evidence to indicate much interest in the legal profession, possibly because he had aspirations for a more active outdoor life. He may not have had the edge to force his way to the top of his chosen career, but would have found his niche in life, where he would have been admired for his personal qualities, regardless of circumstances. If his plans to emigrate to a ranch in Argentina after the war had fallen through, he would have made an excellent diplomat or perhaps a farmer in Herefordshire. If he had found the right person, he would have been an exceptional husband and father. Inevitably this paragraph is all conjecture about a future destined not to be, but it does give some idea of his aspirations for the future – some measure of this promising young man.

*   *   *

Henry was a short, dapper and immaculately dressed man with an air of relaxed bonhomie, while often smoking a cigarette. His ready smile, charm, manners and spontaneous personality were an attractive combination. Throughout most of his life and until his health began to fail, he exuded energy. As is evident in the family group photograph on page 12, Henry had decided to join the Royal Navy from a very young age. Throughout his life he remained single minded, intensely loyal and proud of his achievements in his chosen career. His respect, pride and love for his family came a very close second to his personal ambitions. As he was the only member of his family to join the Royal Navy, it was important to him that his family understood what he was doing and gave him due credit. He was fastidious in his appearance and due to his naval training, extremely tidy. On occasions he reputedly asked that his newspapers be ironed. Although inwardly a serious minded and ambitious sailor, to the outside world he appeared relaxed and wore his naval forage cap at a rakish angle, much in fashion at that time.

When serving in some fourteen seagoing ships, there will have been occasions when his bouts of seasickness, first experienced in HMS *Cumberland* in 1913, were a trial for him. As his health began to deteriorate in 1942, it is likely that these bouts would have become more frequent. By the end of his career he had served in thirteen shore stations. In the latter part of his career, when he was no longer sufficiently robust in health for a seagoing command, the tidy minded aspect of his operational staff officer skills first shown in the 1930s, were put to excellent effect during preparations for D day and for the Rhine crossing. These appointments will have called for sheer determination and energetic leadership at a time when tuberculosis was beginning to take its toll.

There is no doubt that his lifelong friendship with Prince Albert/King George VI was a matter of great pride to him. He guarded this privilege and would not divulge any confidences. He would have been appalled by the modern inclination to leak such confidences to the press. Very much later in life, when in correspondence with John Wheeler-Bennett, who had been commissioned by the Royal Family to write the King's biography, Henry wrote to him on 7 October 1953:

In view of the fact that all the enclosed letters were written privately to me I would prefer you not to mention my name as the person addressed, if you wish to quote any part of them in your book.

Henry's privileged position with Royalty may have been envied by some of his superior officers. There is at least a whiff of evidence that this may have worked to his detriment when his confidential reports were drafted in 1943.

In summary Henry was of average intellect which would have curtailed his selection for very high command. He was an able seagoing Captain, who had a flair for ship's gunnery. Yet in retrospect and later in his career, he showed himself to be a more able staff officer, particularly in coordinating landing craft for assault landings. He enjoyed stimulating company and the better things which life had to offer. There was no real sign of any special relationship with any woman in his life but his thirty four years service in the Royal Navy, a third on war service and three quarters spent at sea meant that opportunities were limited. However, social graces in an essentially private man must have been attractive. It is fair to assume that he had some cherished relationships, but preferred to keep them confidential. During his retirement in London when plagued by ill health, his lack of interests other than in the Royal Navy may have been rather limiting for him. Above all else, he gave unstinting, able, loyal and long standing service to his King and Country.

However, he enjoyed his final years spent in the devoted care of his sister Mary in Herefordshire. With his brother Philip, his sister-in-law Grace and his three nieces Pippa, Caro and Anna, up the road at Highcroft, he was back with his family again.

* * *

John was a good looking man with striking eyes, an infectious smile and a sense of fun. Much broader than his two elder brothers he stood just under six foot and had a strong physique. He was a keen, robust sportsman being particularly successful as a rugby full back, a fast bowler at cricket and a combative full back at hockey. He was also a good shot. He was compassionate towards those less fortunate than himself and was generous by nature. He was spontaneous in showing his emotions to those he loved and intensely loyal when his family or friends were in difficulties. His strong personality exuded genuine interest and enthusiasm, interspersed as necessary with much charm. He had considerable energy and was determined to live life to the full, regardless of the consequences. He had great pride in his family yet was not averse to being irritated by the foibles of some members. He could occasionally be moody and was inclined to impatience and had a short temper when he could not get his way. He was a natural flirt with good-looking women.

His deep love for his wife and children was paramount in his life. He was an inveterate and proud keeper of family records. Although Davina and I were still very young when he sailed to North Africa in February 1943, we both, even now, are aware of his love for us. Despite the excitement of the war, he longed for peace and to be home again. However our mother, much later in life, always doubted whether after the war John would have had the temperament or patience for soldiering in peacetime.

He was a very able soldier, who by nature was rather impatient and did not suffer fools gladly. He was intellectually rather above average, but his preference for practical matters and his irritation with theory, probably accounted for his failing the Staff College examination. Nevertheless because of the war he, together with several other promising contemporaries, was awarded a vacancy on the short course. He was by nature keen to be at the centre of the action during the war, where he displayed natural leadership skills, calm determination, sound judgement and consistent bravery. As shown in his letter to Henry he had an element of bravado, which was typical of the time and he liked recounting his narrow escapes. By mid 1944 after the battles of Anzio and Cassino had taken their toll, his former youthful dark hair was receding from his temples and going grey. Had he survived the war, many of his contemporaries have told us that he would have been promoted to the highest rank. As with his elder brother Eric, this must remain conjecture.

* * *

All three brothers devoted their lives to the service of their Country during a time of bitter conflict in the world. As a family we are very proud of them – for being such fine yet differing personalities and for doing all they did to safeguard our Country's freedom from oppression. Let us pray that Eric's and John's sacrifice and Henry's lifetime of devoted service were not in vain and that mankind has learned that warfare on this scale must never happen again.

Like so many other families, ours suffered their share of loss during two world wars, yet like the vast majority of others refused to buckle. Invariably it was our womenfolk, who grieved deepest nevertheless proved to be more resilient and steadfast. In our family's case, it was my grandmother Sophie, bereft of her two sons Eric and John, who set the tone.

Davina and I well remember our post war visits to 'Grannie Hereford'. None were complete until she had removed her concertina from its case and invited both of us and our mother to sing *Onward Christian Soldiers*. As lumps in throats subsided so our voices were soon raised in defiant and prideful unison. Our mother, Ann had by then already shown that her generation possessed a different but no lesser blend of courage and stoicism in the face of adversity.

Davina and I, like countless other wartime children who lost their father, reflect sadly on the brevity of our parents' time together. Their sacrifice gave us both the opportunity much later in our lives to enjoy long and happy marriages. But John and Anne had been married less than six years when war broke out, were only married for ten and a half years when John was killed. Nineteen months of this time John was away fighting.

One of Anne's favourite books which she passed on to me was *The White Cliffs* by Alice Duer Miller. Verse XL must have struck a chord:

As I grow older, looking back, I see
Not those the longest planted in the heart
Are the most missed. Some unions seem to be
Too close for even death to tear apart.
Those who have lived together many years
And deeply learnt to read each other's mind,
Vanities, tempers, virtues, hopes and fears –
One cannot go – nor is one left behind.
Alas, with John and me this was not so:
I was defrauded even of the past.
Our days had been so pitifully few,
Fight as I would, I found the dead go fast.
I had lost all – had lost not love alone,
But the bright knowledge it had been my own.

Field of Remembrance

As is well known, every late October and early November, under the direction of The Royal British Legion Poppy Appeal, crosses manufactured by The RBL Poppy Factory are bought by the public. During Remembrance Day, many people quietly plant their crosses in their local War Memorial Garden in memory of their loved ones killed in either World War or in any subsequent conflict. At about 10.50am brief Services of Dedication and Remembrance take place throughout the United Kingdom and Commonwealth. A Bugler sounds 'Last Post' before the two minutes silence, then 'Reveille' to signal our return to the bustle of daily life.

Less well known is the Field of Remembrance at St Margaret's Westminster in London. In 1928 Major George Howson MC began the tradition of the Royal British Legion Poppy Staff organising a Field of Remembrance in the grounds of Westminster Abbey to allow passers-by to

89. KSLI Plot at the Field of Remembrance 2003

plant commemorative crosses to honour the Fallen. From this simple start the Field has developed into a national event. The Service of Dedication and Remembrance, invariably attended by Her Majesty the Queen, marks the Opening of the Field of Remembrance. In 2004 there were 246 representative memorial plots into which crosses were placed, resulting in a donation of just under £24,000 towards the Poppy Appeal. Plot No 38 is allocated to The King's Shropshire Light Infantry and The Herefordshire Regiment.

Recently it has been my privilege to lay out our Regimental Plot in readiness for this Service of Remembrance. When Christopher Cotterell, who had carried out this task with devotion for fifteen years, died in November 2002, it seemed right to offer my services.

At the going down of the sun and in the morning,
  We will remember them.

Family Acknowledgements

My sister, Davina Vickers
for her vivid recall of episodes which typified our father, John and our Uncle Henry. Our searches through family albums have brought back so many memories of our early childhood and of our remarkable parents. Her spontaneous enthusiasm - inherited from John - has been an inspiration.

My cousin, June Robertson
has written two books, *A Long Way from Tipperary* and very recently *Only Remember the Laughter*. Like me, she has taken to writing late in life and knows only too well the challenge of producing family histories (in her case, of her father's Carrol family). Being in the same boat, it has been fun encouraging each other. June inherited many of Henry's papers and promptly handed these over to me. She also loaned her parents' photograph album. Her descriptions of her two uncles, Henry and John, reflect her love for her family and her light touch.

My cousins, Pippa Boast, Caro Jones and Anna Knight
to whom I sent an early extract relating to their father, Philip and their Uncle Henry. They gathered together and spent a happy and nostalgic day reminiscing. Pippa, the eldest, acted as editor, researcher and provider of information on Philip and also recounted their memories of Henry. Some

years ago, Caro kindly sent me Eric's *In Memoriam* booklet, lovingly compiled by his parents. Recently Caro arranged for the family grave at Tupsley in Hereford to be repaired, cleaned and photographed.

My cousin, Margaret Spencer
is the eldest daughter of Harold, my Grandfather's eldest son. She is now the senior original Gwynne-James. When I sent her an extract regarding our family, she gladly gave me the information I needed and much encouragement.

My aunt, Mary Rhys
who died in 1969. She was the eldest in the family of eight children and it was she who kept the Family Scrap Book, which I have inherited. Her priceless family archive made *For King and Country* possible. I like to think she would have approved.

My wife, Charmian
for researching her Grandfather's letters from Armentières in 1915, which describe in such understated fashion, life in the trenches which Eric experienced. I am so grateful for her perceptive ideas, genuine interest, encouragement and patience.

Sources and References

Eric
The History of the King's Shropshire Light Infantry in the Great War 1914-1918 edited *by Major W de B Wood*
The King's Shropshire Light Infantry 1881–1968 *compiled by Peter Duckers for the Shropshire Regimental Museum*
Photographs: Officers of the 1st KSLI in France in 1916, page 40
    The 1st Battalion leaving the trenches near Ginchy in 1916, page 43
Official History of The War: Military Operations France and Belgium 1915
    photograph: Hooge 9 August 1915
The Somme *by Garry Sheffield*
The Western Front *by Richard Holmes*
Family Papers

Henry
King George VI His Life and Reign *by John W Wheeler-Bennett*
Part I Prince Albert, 1895–1920

Chapter II. Osborne, Dartmouth and *Cumberland*, 1908–1912
   Osborne House. Description pages 38 to 47
   Henry's friendship with Prince Albert page 41
   What appealed to his five friends including Jimmy James page 42
   Difference between Osborne and Dartmouth page 47
   RNC Dartmouth. Description pages 47 to 59
Chapter III. Naval Career, 1913–1917
   HMS *Collingwood* September 1913–August 1917 pages 66–104
   Midshipman 'lowest form of marine life' page 67
   Known as Mr Johnson page 67
   Description of life aboard HMS *Collingwood* pages 71 – 77
   Appendicitis and various periods of gastric illness pages 77 – 104
   Battle of Jutland May 1916. Henry in Turret 'A'. Prince Albert's account pages 94 – 96

National Archives at Kew; Royal Naval Records
   Statement of Service
   Record of Service ADM 196/118 page 130
   Confidential Report
   Navy Lists
Ships Logs
   ADM 53/38187 Battle of Jutland (May and June 1916)
   ADM 137/3660 Collision HMS *Redoubt* and Coal Hulk *Himalaya* (18/4/1917)
   ADM 1/8591/116 Report on Cadet Training Cruise HMS *Temeraire* (6–12/1920)
   ADM/267/69 HMS *Capetown* Henry's report to Enquiry on Torpedo incident 1/5/1941 and photographs of damage. Report of Findings of Court of Enquiry (3/6/1941).
   ADM 1/11175 HM Ships–Damage and Loss. HMS *Capetown* recovery to Bombay
   ADM 1/30174 Award of DSC to 3 officers for assault on Walcheren 11/1944
   ADM 179/535 Force U for Rhine crossing 1945
   ADM 1/19168 Operation Banknote (Crossing the Rhine)
Ships Photographs
   ADM 176/ 142 HMS *Collingwood*
   ADM 176/ 698 HMS *Temeraire*
   ADM 176/ 260 HMS *Fearless*
   ADM 267/ 69 No 2 HMS *Capetown* Views of hole from dockside looking forward

National Maritime Museum; *Caird Library, at Greenwich*
Ships Histories
  HMS *Redoubt* Sopwith Camel shoots down Zeppelin (18/8/1918)
  HMS *Versatile* Cruise routes 1924 and 1925
  HMS *Fearless* anti piracy patrol and evacuation of refugees off Spain
  1936–1938
  HMS *Capetown* torpedoed 8/4/1941
Ships movements
  HMS *Capetown* 30/11/1940–6/1941
  HMS *Capetown* 17/7/1942–14/11/1942
Navy Lists
Images of Royal Navy cap badge and insignia of ADC to the King

Ships of the Royal Navy *by JJ Colledge*
  HMS Ships specifications and armaments
A Dictionary of Ships of the Royal Navy of the Second World War *by John Young*
  HMS Ships specifications and armaments
Chronology of the War at Sea 1939–1945 *by J Rohwer & G Hummelchen*
  HMS *Capetown* supports advance against Italian Somaliland
  10–12/2/1941
  HMS *Capetown* action East Africa/Red Sea 1–8/4/1941
  Operation Infatuate (Walcheren) 1/11/1944
This Great Harbour Scapa Flow *by WS Hewison*
  Description of harbour and HMS Iron Duke March–September 1943
The Encyclopedia of Code Names of World War II *by Christopher Cant*
  Overlord/Neptune (Normandy)
  Infatuate (Walcheren)
  Banknote (Rhine Crossing)
Shore Establishments of the Royal Navy *by Lieutenant Commander B Warlow RN*
  HMS *Pembroke* 1932 -1933
  Massawa Naval Repair Base 7/1941–9/1941
  Trincomalee Ceylon 12/1941–2/1942
  HMS *Iron Duke* 3/1943–7/1943
  HMS *Proserpine* 7/1943–11/1943
  HMS *Squid* 1/1944–2/1945
  HMS *Stag* 6/1945–1/1946
The Longest Day *by Cornelius Ryan*
Gold Beach Battle Zone Normandy *by Simon Trew*
  Photograph; Force G landing craft at Southampton 1st June 1944 page 46
Family Papers

John

1st Battalion The King's Shropshire Light Infantry Campaign Service 1939–1945 (France–Belgium–North Africa–Italy) *compiled by Lieutenant Colonel R Evans MC, Late KSLI and Maurice E Jones, Late KSLI*

Propaganda leaflet dropped by German aircraft in May 1940 page 18

Photograph. Bugle Platoon 1 KSLI 1942 page 28

North Africa and Pantelleria March–December 1943 pages 29–42

Anzio Assault Landing 22 January–7 March 1944 pages 43–69

Anzio from 8 March 1944 to the Fall of Rome pages 70–82

The Nine Days Wonder (Operation Dynamo) *by John Masefield*

The First Division in Action, Tunisia 1943

Image of 1st Division flash

Sketch Map. The Advance from Medjez 23rd April–6th May 1943

1st Bn The King's Shropshire Light Infantry Notes: 'An authentic account of our doings' in North Africa

Imperial War Museum; Photograph Archive

NA 2605 KSLI soldiers talking to Arabs beside a knocked out German tank at Tebourba 8th May 194

NA 14222 Brigadier John Gwynne-James addressing NCOs at a Course of Instruction after cessation of hostilities in Tunisia 1943

NA 3590 Admiral Pavesi of the Italian Navy and his Chief of Staff at Pantelleria June 1943

Imperial War Museum; Department of Printed Books

Pantelleria. The Reduction of Pantelleria and Adjacent Island 8th May–14th June 1943. *Army Air Force History Study 52.*

Sketch Map. Pantelleria Island showing coastal defences page 5

The Trasimene Line June–July 1944 by Janet Kinrade Dethick.

Sketch Maps:

No 6. 20th–21st June 1944 Villastrada–Vaiano

No 8. 24th June–1st July 1944 Pescia River–Spina River

No 9. Detailed Troop Movements 24th–29th June 1944 Pescia River

Shropshire Regimental Museum

Image of KSLI Cap badge

The Iron Duke, the Magazine of The Duke of Wellington's Regiment, October 1943

Personal impressions of the Bou Aoukaz Action 5th and 6th May 1943 pages 86 – 92

Pantelleria 11th June 1943 pages 92–94

articles by Lieutenant Colonel Brian W Webb-Carter, CO 1st Bn The Duke of Wellington's Regiment

Why the White Flag went up on Pantelleria *by Alexander Clifford*
Extract from his dispatches.

Anzio *by Wynford Vaughan-Thomas*
1 Prologue. Sketch Map. Stalemate in Italy December 1943 page 13
4 The Landing
5 Advance at last. Sketch Map. The Advance to Campoleone 29th–30th January 1944 page 77
6 Lancing the abscess. Sketch Map. First German counter-attack on British 1st Division 3rd–4th February 1944, page 99

Cassino Portrait of a Battle *by Fred Majdalany*
The Fourth Battle
Sketch Map. Fifth and Eighth Armies break through and begin successful advance to Rome page 229

Alex The Life of Field Marshal Earl Alexander of Tunis *by Nigel Nicholson*
10 Alexander of Tunis
12 Salerno and Anzio.
Sketch Map. Anzio 22nd–23rd January 1944 page 179

The Memoirs of Field Marshal Earl Alexander of Tunis 1940–1945 *edited by John North*
IV 'Torch pays off'
X The War in Italy

Desert Generals *by Corelli Barnett*
Appendix C Major General E Dorman-Smith page 308

War in Italy 1943–1945 *by Field Marshal Lord Carver*
6 Break through to Rome May to June 1944
7 Push to Florence June to August 1944

Algiers to Austria A History of the 78th Division in the Second World War *by Cyril Ray*
April through June 1944
Page 150 Action 25th and 26th June 1944

War Diaries 78th Division and 36th Infantry Brigade
Action at bridgehead over the River Pescia 26th June 1944

Pippin's Progress A Soldier Artist's War *by Richard Heseltine*
7 Orvieto pages 204 and 205

Alexander's Generals The Italian Campaign 1944–1945 *by Gregory Blaxland*
Page 150 Action 25th and 26th June 1944

The White Cliffs *by Alice Duer Miller*, verse XL

Family Papers

Notes

Eric

1. It was a coincidence to discover that my wife's maternal grandfather, Guy Goodliffe, who wrote regular letters home from the trenches to his wife, Grace, was serving in the trenches at Armentières at the same time as Eric. It was remarkable to discover that Eric's riflemen took over the trenches from Guy's fusiliers in early January 1915. As no letters home from Eric now exist, it seems appropriate to rely on extracts from Guy's letters to describe the scenes at the time.
2. DSO (Distinguished Service Order); MC (Military Cross); MM (Military Medal); DCM (Distinguished Conduct Medal).
3. This photograph was probably taken near St Omer in July 1916 before the Battalion moved to the Somme.

Henry

4. Passing out examinations from R N C Dartmouth.
5. This statement that the last part of the Cruise would be spent in the Mediterranean was incorrect. After the West Indies and Bermuda, the *Cumberland* proceeded to Halifax, Quebec etc.
6. Henry's comment to John Wheeler-Bennett was: 'I do not remember the smoking incident, but my guess is that possibly some Cadets were spotted smoking in one of the Ship's boats. Smoking by Cadets was prohibited and nobody is allowed to smoke in a Ship's boat. HM's remark gives you an idea of his dislike of indiscipline.'
7. Henry's comment to John Wheeler-Bennett was: 'Jack Briggs was a very charming fellow in our Term and who evidently HM hoped very much to have with us in the *Collingwood*. Unfortunately he was killed in World War I – I think in Minesweepers.'
8. Henry's comments and explanation to John Wheeler-Bennett were: 'I think you will agree that this is a thoroughly interesting, human and charming letter, which clearly shows his constant thought for others and strong sense of duty.'
   'Talbot (para 6) was his Marine Servant.'
   'Tait (para 7) was then Lieutenant Tait, who was responsible for the Midshipmen's Instruction in the *Collingwood*. Later in his career, as Sir William Tait, he was Commander in Chief, South Africa Station. He died a few years ago, when he was, I think, Governor of Southern Rhodesia, but that would need checking.'
   'Philpotts (par 7, last line) was the Gunroom Messman.'
9. October 28 1915, while inspecting men of the 1st Wing of the Royal Flying Corps at Hesdigneul in France, King George met with a serious accident. His horse took fright at the cheers, and, rearing, fell backwards, pinning the King under her. His Majesty received serious injuries.'
10. Henry's comment and explanation to John Wheeler-Bennett were: 'Another very natural and charming letter written while he was still ashore, which again shows his eagerness to get back to the Grand Fleet.'

'Avery (para 1) was Naval Instructor with us in the *Cumberland* and responsible for our instruction in Navigation.'

'Tait (para 6) is same person as that referred to in my remarks concerning HM's letter dated 30th October 1914 (8).'

'Sir S Colville (para 6) was the then Vice Admiral Sir Stanley Colville, Home Fleet. When World War I started, *Collingwood* became a private ship, but still remained in the First Battle Squadron. Admiral Colville became Admiral Commanding Orkneys and Shetlands. Later, I think he became Commander in Chief, Portsmouth and it must be to getting that appointment that HM refers in his sentence – He is very sick about Portsmouth... Admiralty.'

'Cavendish (final para) is G S G Cavendish, who was in our Term and a nephew, I think, of the then Duke of Devonshire.'

11. Henry's explanation to John Wheeler-Bennett regarding the 'confidential job' referred to in the first line of paragraph 2 of the above letter was:

'It was while I was temporarily serving in *Foxglove* that I received a letter, which was signed by Hampden (I forget his rank) at the Admiralty asking me if I would volunteer for a secret active service job. It directed me to reply by telegram and, in the event of my volunteering, I would be directed to report to the Admiralty where I would receive further details. In my eagerness and with the concurrence of the commanding officer, *Foxglove* (Lieutenant Commander Hermon-Hodge) I gladly volunteered. However, on second thoughts, it occurred to me that, to be loyal to my proper Captain (Captain J C Ley of *Collingwood*), I should really get his permission before volunteering. So I saw Captain Ley and explained the situation. The result was that he regretfully forbade me to volunteer, giving as his reason that I was too valuable in the *Collingwood*, as at that time my Action Station was Commanding Officer of a Twin 12 inch Turret – a job I knew thoroughly. A great disappointment! I discovered later that the secret job was Coastal Motorboats – a service that the Admiralty was just starting. They were high speed craft which did excellent work against the Germans on the Belgian Coast.'

'Jimmy (para 2) was of course Captain James C Ley of *Collingwood*.'

'Turnour (para 2) was in our Term and joined *Collingwood* with us.'

'Christie (para 3) was the senior Sub Lieutenant of the Gunroom. Greig (para 6) was a charming fellow, who HM greatly liked. He joined the RAF with HM and had a lot to do with him in many ways. He later became Sir Louis Grieg.'

12. Bertrand Dawson was the King's Surgeon.

13. In the course of the Battle of Verdun, which lasted from February 21 to December 20, 1915, the German losses were 336,831.

14. Henry's explanations to John Wheeler-Bennett were: 'During the latter part of 1916 my own brother (Eric), who was Adjutant of the King's Shropshire Light Infantry, was badly wounded and eventually died in Hospital at Rouen. It was because of my eagerness to have a crack at the Germans as a result of that, the fact that it seemed unlikely that the German High Sea Fleet would risk another major engagement, and also the fact that HM had left the *Collingwood*, that I wrote to HM asking him if he could possibly get me appointed to a destroyer in the Harwich Striking Force. The result was this charming letter.'

'Buller (para 1) was the Commander at RNC Dartmouth when we were there. When the letter was written, he was Naval Assistant to the Second Sea Lord. He later, I think, became Admiral in command of HM Yachts.'

'Harries (para 3) was at one time a sub lieutenant in the Gunroom. He later went in for flying.'

'AK Gibson (para 3) was a Lieutenant in the *Cumberland* during our Training Cruise.'

'Nicholson (para 4) was Captain Ley's relief in command of the *Collingwood*.'

15. It was only after my researches in Ships Histories at the Public Record Office had highlighted this action involving HMS *Redoubt*, that I returned home to discover by coincidence this piece of fabric tucked away in a wallet file among some family papers.

16. Henry's explanation to John Wheeler-Bennett was: 'After World War I, I was appointed to HMS *Cornwall*, one of the two cadet training Cruisers – the other being the *Cumberland*. Thus the reason for my having written from Sydney, Cape Breton Island, which was one of the places visited during the Training Cruise.'

17. Henry wrote: 'Rolleston and Herbert (para 3) were officers in the *Collingwood* with us.'

18. Henry wrote: 'Although I do not remember, I have no doubt that this letter led to one of the occasions on which I had lunch with HM at Buckingham Palace.'

19. Massawa was the one time pearl of the Red Sea – the hub of ancient trading routes.

20. By coincidence, those units aboard Force G landing craft bound for the assault at Arromanches on 6th June, included the 2nd Devons, under command of Lieutenant Colonel Cosmo Nevill. He was to be awarded an immediate DSO for his leadership before being seriously wounded on 16th July 1944. Twenty one years later in 1965, a few years after a heart attack had forced him into early retirement as a Major-General, I became happily married to his daughter, Charmian.

21. My researches have failed to discover what Henry was doing during his two months with HMS *Odyssey* ,which was a Naval Pay Accounting Base quartered in the Collingwood Hotel in Ilfracombe.

John

22. Although I played a dozen times at Lords and hit several sixes, I failed to emulate his towering hit.

23. According to my mother, when John was faced with an examination question which he could not answer, he wrote about bodyline bowling – highly topical after Douglas Jardine's Ashes Tour of Australia in 1933.

24. The guidon of the Island of Pantelleria is on display at the Shropshire Museum in Shrewsbury.

25. The Italians had left their surrender so late that our invasion had to roll on for some time by its own momentum. The bombing programme was dragged finally to a halt, but not before several Italian positions had been raided superfluously and Admiral Pavesi, apparently bewildered by the situation, fled into the hills. The commander sent an emissary with an interpreter to chase him, and finally he consented to walk down to the airfield. There – a handsome, elderly man with grey hair and plenty of gold braid on his uniform – he waited with General Maffei. They gasped with astonishment when the British General (John) drove up in a tank; they had never dreamed that tanks could be got ashore so swiftly and manoeuvred up to the airfield. (Dispatches of Alexander Clifford of the British Press)

26 On 24 June 217 BC on the northern shore of Lake Trasimene, the Carthaginian leader Hannibal destroyed a Roman army of 25,000 men after ambushing them under cover of mist.

27. It seems that John may have reverted to Brigade Commander at this stage.

Index

Bold figures *indicate illustration page numbers*

Adolf Hitler Line 162–3
Albert Line 170–1, 175
Albert, Prince (Mr Johnson) (later King
    George VI)
    appendicitis 66, 67, 68
    becomes King 91–2
    Henry appointed ADC 112
    HMS *Collingwood* 62–6, **65**, 68, 72, 73–6
    HMS *Cumberland* 59, 60
    letters to Henry
        Christmas Card (1920-21) **82**, 83
        HMS *Collingwood* 62–3, 64, 67–72, 75–6, 210
        HMS *Cumberland* 58
        HMS *Redoubt* 78
        Prince George joins ship 79–80, 81–2
        publication 55, 57, 199
        wishes speedy recovery 102
    Royal Naval College Dartmouth **56**, 57, 58
    Royal Naval College Osborne 54, 55, 57
    telegrams to Henry 92, **93**, **117**
Anzio 146–50, **148**, 157–8, 180
Arbuthnot, Admiral 103
Arkwright family, memories of Eric 52
Armentières 25–8, 209
Avery, Naval Instructor 69, 210
Aylestone Hill
    Eric 50
    family home 11, 13, **14**, 124, 192, 193
    Henry **89**
    John and June **127**
    Sophie and John **126**, **129**
    Sophie's role 122, 124

Baillie, Lady Helena 121
Barnett, Corelli 158, 159, 208
Beatty, Sir David 73
Biddy **128**
Blaxland, Gregory 176
Boast, Pippa (née Gwynne-James),
    memories 122, 199, 203
Bordon, Hampshire 131, 183, 189
Bou Aoukaz, Battle for 136, 138, 140
Brand, Captain 71
Briggs, Jack 63, 209
British Army
    in France
        WWI **27**, 38–40
        WWII, B.E.F. 132–3, 135
    in Italy
        1st Infantry Division 149, 150, 151, 154, 156
        36th Infantry Brigade 157, 158–60, 165–7,
            170–3, 176, 187–8
Broadhead, P.M. 95, 97
Buckley, F.A. 107
Buist, Colin 55
Buller, Naval Assistant 76, 210

Camberley, Staff College 132, 184
Campbell, H.G. 92

Campoleone Salient 150–6, **152**, **155**
Careless, Colonel 'Bunny' 158, 159–60
Carrington, Charles 39–40
Carroceto, defence 156–7
Carver, Field Marshal Lord 158, 208
Cassino 158–63, **163**, 182, 184
Castiglione del Lago **174**, 175, 176
Cavan, Lieutenant General Lord 33–4
Cavendish, G. 55, 70, 71, 76, 82, 210
Chateau des Trois Tours 32–3
Chatham 88–9, 104, 112, 116
Cheltenham College 22–3, **23**, **44**, 45, **45**
Christian, Captain 54
Christie, Senior Sub Lt 71, 72, 210
Cimbano, Battle for 171–5, **172**
Clark, General Mark 157, 163–4
Colchester 130, 183
Collins, Captain H.S. 41–2
Colville, Vice-Admiral Stanley 64, 70
Cotterell, Christopher 203
Culley, Lieutenant S.D. 77, **77**, 78
Curzon of Kedlestone, Earl 80

D-Day 105–6, 107, 180, 182, 189–90
Daily Telegraph 32–3
Danesmere 122
Dartmouth, Royal Naval College 57–63
Dawson, Bertrand 72, 210
Devizes, Senior Officers School 135
Dix-Perkin, Lieutenant Colonel 193–4
Dobie, Mr L.J. (headmaster) 22, 52
Donaldson, Captain L. 80
Dorman-Smith, Major General 158–60, 208
Duke of Kent *see* George, Prince
Duke of Wellington's Regiment 136, 138, 143,
    151, 154, 167, 207–8
Duke of York *see* Albert, Prince
Dunkirk 133, 135, 189, 194
Dynes, Major Ernest 194–5

Evans, Captain E.R.G. 81
Evans, Lieutenant Colonel Dick 135

Farnham, Littlegates 131, 189, 190, 194
Findlay, M. de C. 80–1
Fleurs-Courcelette, Battle of 35–7, 75
Force U 108–11, **108**, **109**, **111**, 116
France
    WWI 25–8, 34–40
    WWII 131–5

George, Prince (Duke of Kent) 79, 80–1
George V, King 64, 66, 69
George, VI, King *see* Albert, Prince
Gibson, Lieutenant A.K. 76, 211
Godfrey, Mr (headmaster) 54
Goodliffe, Capt Guy 25–6, 28, 29–30, 209
Gray, Mr and Mrs E.F. 80–1
Grieg, Louis 71, 210
Gustav Line 146, **147**, 150, 158, 182
Gwynne-James & Sons 11, 18, 20

Gwynne-James family
  family grave **51**, 204
  family tree 11
  memories of Eric 50, 52, 197–8
  memories of Henry 120–2, 198–9, 203
  memories of John 189–95, 199–200
  motto 2
  twins 11, 124
Gwynne-James, Anna *see* Knight, Anna
Gwynne-James, Anne **127**
  at Buckingham Palace **178**
  with Davina **131**
  death 195
  engagement/marriage **129**, 130
  with John **127**
  John's death 190, 191, 192, 201
  letters from John 167, 169, 170, 175–6
  memories of John 193, 200
  Remembrance Services 18
Gwynne-James, Arthur (1855–1936) 20, 45
Gwynne-James, Caro *see* Jones, Caro
Gwynne-James, Charmian 18, 211
Gwynne-James, David
  at Buckingham Palace **178**
  Cheltenham College 45
  childhood 130
  family memories 18–19, 200–1
  with father **131**
  with father and grandfather **134**
  KSLI 43
  memories of father 189, 190, 192, 193
  memories of Henry 120–2
  postcards from father 195
  tonsils 175, 191–2
Gwynne-James, Davina *see* Vickers, Davina
Gwynne-James, Eric 'Jimmy' (1893–1916) **21**, **24**
  affection for Mary 32, 46–7
  awards/medals 30, 33, 37, 38
  Cheltenham College 22–3, 45
  childhood/early life **12**, 22–5
  death 37, 38, 52, 75
  family memories 50, 52, 197–8, 204
  grave **42**, 43
  with Henry and Lord James **23**
  KSLI
    Adjutant 30, 33, 34, **34**, 37, 38, 41
    Armentières 25–8
    Flers-Courcelette 35–7, 75
    joins up 25
    Rifle Platoon Commander 34
    Second Lieutenant 25
    Somme, Battle of the 34–5
    Ypres Salient 28–34
  letters to Henry 31–2, 46–8
  letters to Tina 31
  memorials 43, **45**
  in Memoriam letters 40–3, 204
  Oriel College 23, **24**, 25, 197
  WWI involvement 15, 25–43
Gwynne-James, Frank James (Francis Reginald
    James)
  Cheltenham College 45
  family home 11
  Golden Wedding Day **17**
  Gwynne-James & Sons 18, 124
  links with Hereford 20
  marriage 13
  visits Eric in hospital 52

Gwynne-James, Grace 122, 199
Gwynne-James, Harold (1893–1964) **12**, 13, 18, 20,
    45, 52
Gwynne-James, (Percival) Henry (Henny)
    'Jimmie' (1896–59) **53**, **113**
  affection for John 121
  appointed ADC to King 112
  childhood/early life **12**, 54–8
  death 122
  effect of Eric's death 75, 210
  Eric, letters from 31–2
  with Eric and Lord James **23**
  family memories 120–2, 198–9, 203
  health problems 102, 103–4, 105, 112, 114, 116,
    122, 198
  hears of John's death 106
  letter from John 138–41
  letter to parents 84
  lost papers 55, 83
  with Mary and John **83**
  with mother and grandfather **87**
  Prince Albert
    friendship 54, 55, 57, 70–1, 198–9, 210
    letters from 55, 57, 58, 62–3, 64, 67–72, 76, 78,
      79–80, 81, 102, 199, 210
    telegrams from 92, **93**, **117**
  Royal Navy
    appointed Captain 92, 115, 116
    appointed Commander 88, **89**, 115, 116
    appointed Director of Personal Services 89,
      116
    appointed first command 84
    appointed Lieutenant 76, 78, 115
    appointed Midshipman 60–1, **61**, 62, 115
    appointed Naval Officer i/c Trincomalee
      102, 103, 114, 116
    appointed Sub Lieutenant 72, 115
    Court of Enquiry 99–101, 103, **118–20**
    discharge 112, 116
    Force U Commander 108–11, **109**, **111**, 116
    HMS *Antelope* 87, 88, **88**, 115
    HMS *Capetown* 95, **96**, 97–104, **100**, 114, 116,
      118–20
    HMS *Colleen* 83, 115
    HMS *Collingwood* 62–70, 72, 73–6, 115, 209,
      210, 211
    HMS *Cumberland* 58–63, 94, 209, 210, 211
    HMS *Fearless* 89–92, **90**, 116
    HMS *Foxglove* 70, 71, 72, 115, 210
    HMS *Iron Duke* 104–5, 116, 138
    HMS *Landseer* 108–9
    HMS *Mackay* 92, 116
    HMS *Odyssey* 111, 116, 211
    HMS *Pembroke* 88–9, 116
    HMS *Proserpine* 104, 116
    HMS *Redoubt* 76–8, 115, 211
    HMS *Shakespeare* 84, 115
    HMS *Squid* 105–7, 116
    HMS *Stag* 112, 116
    HMS *Stormcloud* 84–7, **85**, 115
    HMS *Temeraire* 78–83, **79**, 115
    HMS *Vancouver* 83, 115
    HMS *Versatile* 83, 115
    Operations Division 92, 116
    personal significance 198
    Royal Naval College Dartmouth 57–63, 79
    Royal Naval College Osborne 54–5
    Shanghai, Naval Liaison Officer **93**, 94–5, 97, 116

shore appointments 88–9, 92, 102–12, 116, 211
Statement of Service 115–16
WWI involvement 15, 66–78, 115
WWII involvement 15, 94–114, 116
Gwynne-James, Henry Percival (d.1903) 45
Gwynne-James, John (1820-1908) 20
Gwynne-James, John (1903-1944) **123**, **179**
36th Infantry Brigade 157–60, 165–7, 170, 171, 173, 176, 184, 187, 188
with Biddy **128**
Cheltenham College 45, 124–5, **126**
childhood/early life **12**, 124–5
children 130–1, **131**, 200
death 106, 159–60, 176–8, 194–5
DSO award 136, **178**, **185**
family memories 189–95, 199–200
Farnham home 131
with father and David **134**
grave 178, 180, **181**
health 124
hears of Eric's death 52, 124
with Henry and Mary **83**
Henry's affection for 121
Italian campaign 149–78, 194
KSLI
1st Battalion 135, 183, 184, 189
2nd Battalion 130, 183
3rd Infantry Brigade 131, 136, **139**, 141, 143, 149–60, **152**, **155**
11th Infantry Brigade 130
Anzio 149–50, 184
appointed Adjutant 130, 183
appointed Assistant Brigade Major 133
appointed Brigadier 136–41
appointed Commanding Officer **134**, 135, 184, 189
appointed General Staff Officer 132, 135, 184
appointed Instructor, Senior Officers School 135, 184
appointed Lieutenant Colonel **134**, 135
appointed Major 135
appointed Staff Captain 130
Beauman Division 133
Bugle Platoon **134**
India 129–30, 183
joins up 125
North African Campaign 135–41, 184
Pantelleria 143, **144**, **145**, 184
pre-war service 129–31
WWII service 15, 18, 131–88
letter to Henry 138–41
letters to Anne 167, 169, 170, 175–6
letters to children 195
marriage **129**, 130
with mother **126**, **129**
Royal Navy interest 64, 124
Sandhurst RMC 125, **125**, 183
Statement of Service 183–4
Gwynne-James, Kington (1730-1787) 20
Gwynne-James, Margaret see Spencer, Margaret
Gwynne-James, Mary see Rhys, Mary
Gwynne-James, Philip (1899-1982) **12**
Cheltenham College 45
Gwynne-James & Sons 18, 20
links with Hereford 20
memories of Henry 122, 199, 203
WWI service 13
WWII service 13

Gwynne-James, Pippa see Boast, Pippa
Gwynne-James, Sophie
with children **12**
with Eric **24**
family home 11, 122, 124
Golden Wedding Day **17**
with Henry **61**, **87**
interests 124
with John **126**, **129**
loss of sons 200–1
marriage 13
memories of John 193
visits Eric in hospital 52
Gwynne-James, Surgeon (1756-1801) 20
Gwynne-James, Surgeon (1786-1812) 20
Gwynne-James, Tina (1899-1984) **12**, 31, 50, 52, 190–1, 193
Gwynne-James, Trill (Lilian) (1903-1977) **12**, 13, 20, 124

Haakon, King of Norway 80, 81
Haig, Sir Douglas 33, 35
Hampden 71, 72, 210
Harries, Sub Lieutenant 76, 210
Harrow-on-the-Hill, Henry's home 122
Heatherdown Preparatory School 192
Herbert (HMS *Collingwood*) 82, 211
Hereford, family links 11, 20, 122
Herzeele 33
Heseltine, Major Richard 169–70, 208
Highcroft 122, 199
HMS *Antelope* 87, 88, **88**, 115
HMS *Capetown* 95, **96**, 97–104, **100**, 114, 116, **118–20**
HMS *Colleen* 83, 115
HMS *Collingwood* 62–6, **65**, 68, 70–6, 81, 115, 209, 210, 211
HMS *Cumberland* 58–63, 69, 94, 209, 210, 211
HMS *Fearless* 89–92, **90**, 116
HMS *Foxglove* 70, 71, 72, 115, 210
HMS *Foxhound* 90
HMS *Hampshire* 75
HMS *Iron Duke* 104–5, 116, 138
HMS *Landseer* 108–9
HMS *Mackay* 92, 116
HMS *Odyssey* 111, 116, 211
HMS *Pembroke* 88–9, 116
HMS *Proserpine* 104, 116
HMS *Redoubt* 76–8, 115, 211
HMS *Shakespeare* 84, 115
HMS *Squid* 105–7, **106**, 116
HMS *Stag* 112, 116
HMS *Stormcloud* 84–7, **85**, 115
HMS *Temeraire* 78–83, **79**, 115
HMS *Vancouver* 83, 115
HMS *Versatile* 83, 115
Holmes, Richard 34
Holt, Lieutenant Commander R.V. 77
Hong Kong, piracy 84, 86
Hooge 30, **31**
Horsfall, Colonel John 173
Hythe, Westcliffe Hall Hotel 105

India, John's service **126**, 129–30, 183
Ireland 135
Italy
Adolf Hitler Line 162–3
Albert Line 170–1, 175
Anzio, assault 146–50, **148**, 157–8

campaign strategy 180, 182
Campoleone Salient 150–6, **152**, **155**
Carroceto, defence 156–7
Cassino 158–63, **163**, 182
Cimbano/Villastrada/Vaiano 171–5, **172**
climate and terrain 180
Gustav Line 146, **147**, 150, 182
Rome
    approach towards 150, 163–7
    to Lake Trasimene 167–78, **168**

Jalapahar, Bengal **126**, 130
James of Hereford, Lord (Henry James) 11, 20, **23**, 45
James, John (Solicitor) (1782-1850) 20
Jellicoe, Sir John 73, 104
Johnson, Mr see Albert, Prince
Jones, Caro (née Gwynne-James) 122, 199, 203, 204
Jutland, Battle of 73–6, 104

Keightley, Major General Charles F. 160, 161, 166, 187, 188
King's Shropshire Light Infantry (KSLI)
    1st Battalion 25, 28, **34**, **36**, 129, 130, 133, 135, 136, **138**,183, 189
    2nd Battalion 130, 183
    3rd Battalion 25
    3rd Infantry Brigade 131, 136, **139**, 141, 143, 149–60, **152**, **155**
    4th Division 132–3
    6th Corps, Ireland 135
    11th Infantry Brigade 130
    Armentières 25–8
    Beauman Division 133
    Bugle Platoon **134**
    David's service 43
    Eric's WWI service 15, 25, 30–7
    Field of Remembrance 18, **202**, 203
    Flers-Courcelette, Battle of 35–7
    John's service
        joins up 125
        pre-war 129–31
        WWII 15, 18, 131–88
    Senior Officers School, Devizes 135
    silver statuettes/badges 43, **49**
    Somme, Battle of the 34–40
    WWI memorial 43
    Ypres Salient 28–34
Kitchener, Lord 75
Knight, Anna (née Gwynne-James), memories 122, 199, 203
KSLI see King's Shropshire Light Infantry

La Brique 30
Lake Trasimene, approach to 167–78, **168**
Landing craft 105–11, **106**, **109**
Lemasurier, Captain J. **111**
Lena, Great Aunt 121
Ley, Capt James 'Jimmy' 63, 64, 71, 210
Littlegates, Farnham 131, 189, 190, 194
Luard, Lieutenant Colonel 32, 34
Luard, Mrs 38
Lucas, Lieutenant General John P. 146, 149, 150, 154, 156, 157–8, 186

Markham, H.B. 107
Masefield, John 135, 207

Massawa 98–101, 103, 114, 116, **118–20**, 211
Maurice, Jack 190
May, Admiral Sir William 59
Medals and awards
    display cabinet 18
    Eric 30, 33, 37, 38, 209
    John 136, **178**, **185**
Medjez 136, **137**, 140
Memorials
    WWI 43, **44**, **45**, 49
    WWII, Field of Remembrance 18, 201–3
Ministry of Defence, Henry's service
    Director of Personal Services 89, 116
    Operations Division 92–3, 116
Moore Darling, Reverend 43, 49–50
Moorland House Preparatory School, Heswall 22, 52, 124
Murray, Lieutenant Colonel B.E. 32, 34, **34**, 37, 38, 42, 43

Nevill, Lieutenant Colonel Cosmo 211
Nicholson, Captain 76, 211
Nicholson, Nigel 157, 208
Nicobar Islands 97, 114
Noble, Admiral Sir Percy 94
North Africa 135–41, 184, 194

The Observer 58–9, 91
O'Carroll Scott, June see Robertson, June
O'Carroll Scott, Tony 190–1, 203
Operation Banknote 108
Operation Dynamo 133
Operation Infatuate 106–7
Operation Overlord (Neptune) 105–6, 107, 116, 189–90
Operation Workshop 143
Oriel College, Oxford, Eric 23–5, 197
Orvieto 167, 169–70, 178, 180, **181**
Osborne House, Royal Naval College 54–5
O'Shea, Jack 194

Pantelleria 141–6, **142**, **144**, **145**, 211
Pavesi, Admiral **144**, **145**, 146, 211
Pembroke Dock 130, 193–4
Penney, Major General 149, 151, 154, 156, 159, 160, 186
Pescia River 173, **174**, 175, 176, **177**
Phelps, L.R. 25
Philpotts (Gunroom Messman) 68, 209
Phipps, Lieutenant William Duncan 55
Piracy 84, 86, 90
Port Said 112, 116
Prince of Wales 57, 64, 69, 74, 78, 82
Propaganda leaflet **132**

Ray, Cyril 162, 166, 208
Red Sea 97–8, 112, 116, 211
Reid, Miles 55
Rhine crossing 108–11, **109**, 116
Rhys, Mary (Frances Mary) (née Gwynne-James) (1889-1969) **12**
    Eric, memories of 52
    Eric, visits in hospital 52
    Eric's affection for 32, 46–7, 48
    family memories 204
    Henry, cares for 122, 199
    with Henry and John **83**
    marriage 20

Red Cross Nurse 13, **17**, 46–7, 48
    scrap book 18, 204
Rhys, Rev. Rowland 20
Ripley, Captain Hugh 146
Robertson, June (née O'Carroll Scott) 18–19, 50,
    52, **87**, **127**, 192–3, 203
Rolleston (HMS *Collingwood*) 81–2, 211
Rome
    approach towards 150, 163–7
    to Lake Trasimene 167–78, **168**
Rouen **39**, 40, **42**, 43, 52
Royal Air Force 77, 78, 133, 135
Royal British Legion Poppy Appeal 201–3
Royal Naval Barracks, Chatham 88–9
Royal Naval College
    Dartmouth 57–63, 79
    Osborne 54–5
Royal Naval Hospital, Chatham 104, 112, 116
Royal Navy
    Henry
        joins up 54, 122, 198
        Statement of Service 115–16
    John's interest 64
    see also HMS...

St Chad's Church, Shrewsbury 43
St Omer 33–4
St Peter's Church, Hereford 43
St Sever Cemetery, Rouen **42**, 43
Sandhurst, RMC 125, **125**, 183
Scapa Flow 72, 73, 75, 80, 104, 116
Shanghai, Henry **93**, 94–5, 97, 116
Sheppard, Lieutenant Commander 95, **96**
Shrewsbury 135, 183, 184
Sicily, invasion 146
Slayter, Bill 55
Smith, Captain Aubrey 59
Somaliland, Italian 97–8
Somme, Battle of the 34–40
Spanish Civil War 90–1
Spencer, Margaret, memories 120, 204
Sport
    Eric 22–5, **23**, **24**, 52
    Henry 54, 68
    John 125, **125**, 129, 130, 199, 211
Sunday Times 110

Taggart, Miss 120
Tait, Lieutenant William 68, 70, 71, 72, 73, 81, **102**,
    209, 210
Talbot, Marine Servant 67, 209
Tanks 35–6, **35**, 135, 136, **138**
Templer, General Sir Gerald 157, 158
Tennant, Captain W.G. 133
Tidnacott 13, **17**, **87**, 120, 124, **127**, 130
The *Times* 88, 92
Tonacombe Manor 13, **15**, **16**, 124
Trenches, WWI 25–6, 28, 29–30, 33
Trincomalee 102, 103, 114, 116
Truscott, General 157, 162, 163, 164
Tupsley Church, Hereford 43, **51**, 204
Turner James, Philip (1789-1860) 20
Turnour 71, 210

Vaiano, Battle for 171–5, **172**
Vaughan-Thomas, Wynford 154, 156, 208
Verity, Commander R.G.A. **111**

Vickers, Davina (née Gwynne-James)
    at Buckingham Palace **178**
    birth 130
    with father **131**
    memories of father 189–90, 192–4, 200, 201, 203
    memories of Henry 120–1, 122
Villastrada, Battle for 171–5, **172**
Von Scheer, Admiral 73

Waddon Martyn, Bill **87**
Waddon Martyn family, home 13, 124
Waddon Martyn, Sophie
    see Gwynne-James, Sophie
Walcheren, Island of 106–7
Wallbank, Colour Sergeant H.A. 40–1
Warner, Charles 192
Webb-Carter, Lieutenant Colonel Brian 136, 138,
    143–6, 167
Wells, Admiral 104–5
Western Morning News 91
Westminster Gazette 117
Wheeler-Bennett, John 57, 198–9, 204, 209, 210,
    211
Whittaker, Lieutenant R.E. **111**
World War I
    Armentières 25–8
    Armistice declared 78
    Eric's service 25–43
    family involvement 13, 15, 19
    Flers-Courcelette, Battle of 35–7
    Henry's service 15, 64–78, 115
    Jutland, Battle of 73–6
    memorials **44**, **45**, 49
    outbreak 64, 66
    Somme, Battle of the 34–40
    Ypres Salient 28–34
World War II
    Anzio assault 146–50, **148**, 157–8
    British Expeditionary Force 132–3, 135
    Campoleone Salient 150–6, **152**, **155**
    Carroceto, defence 156–7
    Cassino 158–63, **163**, 182
    Dunkirk 133, 135
    family involvement 13, 15, **17**, 18, 19
    Field of Remembrance 18, 201–3
    Force U, Rhine Crossing deployment 108–11,
        108, **109**, **111**, 116
    Henry's service 15, 94–114, 116
    Italy, campaign strategy 180, 182
    John's service 15, 18, 131–88
    North African Campaign 135–41
    Operation Banknote 108–11
    Operation Dynamo 133
    Operation Infatuate 106–7
    Operation Overlord (Neptune) 105–6
    Operation Workshop 143
    Outbreak 94
    Pantelleria assault 141–6
    Rome
        approach towards 150, 163–7
        to Lake Trasimene 167–78, **168**
    Victory in Europe 112

Ypres Salient 28–34

Zeppelins 73, 77